...vely ...

for far too long. It has been so... self-evident, but it is nonetheless vital... us an enormous favour in opening a door onto this j... Austen's work. Indeed if we ignore this perspective we will never properly appreciate her writing in its true depth."

Philip Mounstephen, CMS

"'Spirituality' is not a word that Jane Austen would have used, as Paula H... worth is quick to point out. Nevertheless this clear, original, and ...dy brings out the much-neglected spiritual and moral dimension ...usten's work. Hollingsworth offers a fresh reading of the novels ...ores both their moral depth and Austen's gentle awareness of ...! frame within which we live our lives. Given the way so much ...tical discourse secularises the past, it is refreshing to read a book ...so alert and sensitive to Jane Austen's own beliefs and which ...her spiritual insights so richly available to modern readers."

...alcolm Guite, author of *Faith, Hope and Poetry*

'Hollingsworth's study is made with the same careful observation ...sibility as its subject, Jane Austen. Paula opens up the intimate ...ealm of the inner life and sets it in the social context. She illuminates both the texts ...nd the person, and makes a significant contribution to the reader's understanding and enjoyment."

Alison White, Bishop of Hull

THE SPIRITUALITY OF JANE AUSTEN

Paula Hollingsworth

Published by Lion Books
an imprint of
Lion Hudson plc
Wilkinson House, Jordan Hill Road,
Oxford OX2 8DR, England
www.lionhudson.com/lion

ISBN 978 0 7459 6860 5
e-ISBN 978 0 7459 6861 2

First edition 2017

Acknowledgments
Scripture quotation marked "KJV" is taken from the Authorized (King James)
Version: rights in the Authorized Version in the United Kingdom are vested in
the Crown. Reproduced by permission of the Crown's patentee, Cambridge
University Press.
Scripture quotations from the Vulgate Bible were checked at www.vulgate.org
pp. 10, 106, 109, 110, 137, 156, 160: Extract from *A Memoir of Jane Austen and
Other Family Recollections* © 2002 J E Austen-Leigh, reprinted by permission of
Oxford University Press.
pp. 15, 106, 119: Extract from *Jane Austen's Letters* © 2011 Deirdre le Faye,
reprinted by permission of Oxford University Press.
p. 33: Extract from *A History of Jane Austen's Family* © 1988 George Holbert
Tucker, reprinted by permission of Sutton Publishing.

A catalogue record for this book is available from the British Library

Printed and bound in the UK, February 2017, LH26

Dedicated with love
to
Audrey Hollingsworth
1931–1983

CONTENTS

INTRODUCTION:
JANE AUSTEN – A SPIRITUAL
WRITER?

When I mention the words "Jane Austen" and "spirituality" in the same sentence, many people's first response is, "I didn't know she was spiritual," before they then add, "… Mr Collins!" – referring to Jane Austen's wickedly mocking portrayal of a clergyman in *Pride and Prejudice*. Elizabeth Bennet comments to her father, on hearing Mr Collins' words for the first time in his letter to Mr Bennet: "There is something very pompous in his style… Can he be a sensible man?" "No, my dear, I think not" is her father's response. "I have great hopes of finding him quite the reverse. There is a mixture of servility and self-importance in his letter, which promises well. I am impatient to see him." Pompous, servile, and self-important – these are the characteristics of Mr Collins throughout the novel. To some readers of her books, then, it comes as a surprise to learn that a large number of Jane Austen's family, including her father and two of her brothers, were clergymen themselves. Moreover, instead of being offended by her irreverent portrayal of Mr Collins, her family delighted in him. Jane's mother, who was the daughter, the wife, and the mother of clergymen, declared that Mr Collins even outclassed Lady Catherine de Bourgh in being her favourite of all of Jane's characters. An attack on one clergyman (or even more than one, as Austen has others who do not measure up) was not seen, by Jane's family, as an attack on them all, or on the Christian faith in general.

A closer examination of Mr Collins' appearances in the novel, however, reveals that Jane Austen only portrays him in a social role. We see him at evening gatherings, parties, and balls in the town of Meryton, at Mr Bingley's home at Netherfield, and at Rosings, the illustrious home of his redoubtable patron, Lady Catherine. We also see him at home with the Bennet family at Longbourn, and in his own "humble abode", Hunsford Parsonage. Jane Austen never describes him leading services at Hunsford Church, she never mentions the nature of his private prayers, and she does not reveal to us anything about Mr Collins' inner spiritual life.

What then might be the spirituality of his creator, Jane Austen? Behind the many social gatherings, the balls, and the parties in her novels, are there glimpses of a deeper spiritual awareness in her storylines, or in the lives of any of her other characters? And what of Jane Austen herself? Her novels have been constantly in print for the two hundred years since her death in 1817, and they continue to be read and enjoyed by millions of people all around the world. Is there anything of enduring depth in her own life, in her inner spiritual journey, which might correspond to the enduring quality of the writings that she left behind?

The testimony of her nephew James Edward Austen-Leigh is that, in Jane Austen's life and writings, we do find deep spiritual resources, but we need to dig deeply to uncover them. For, in his memoir of his aunt, he wrote:

> *I do not venture to speak of her religious principles: that is a subject on which she herself was more inclined to **think** and **act** than to **talk**, and I shall imitate her reserve; satisfied to have shown how much of Christian love and humility abounded in her heart, without presuming to lay bare the roots whence those graces grew.*[1]

Many of us today, in exploring a person's spirituality, might want to search more widely than the "religious principles" and the specifically *Christian* "love and humility" referred to here by James Austen-Leigh. However, we must proceed with great care in relating the term *spirituality* to Jane Austen. For *spirituality* is not a word that was in common usage in her day; our use of the word and our understanding of its current meaning would not have been part of either her vocabulary or her understanding. The word *spiritual* is often used today where the word *religious* would have been used in Jane Austen's time, but many people today use the word *spiritual* in a broader sense than the word *religious*, which refers to the following of the pathway laid down by a specific world religion. We also need to be aware that Jane Austen, in the context of her times, would use the word *religious* in a narrower sense than we would. Though she would have had an awareness of people of other faiths than Christianity, she would have associated Islam and Hinduism with places and people far away from England. There was a small Jewish population of about twenty-five thousand living in England in the late eighteenth and early nineteenth century, the majority of whom were exiles from Germany and Holland, but they lived predominantly in close-knit communities in London and other large cities. The world in which Jane lived was a very different one from ours, so we have to be careful not to impose a modern, global, multi-religious world view on her novels and experience.

So, to Jane Austen, the word *religious* would have meant Christian. Furthermore, it would have meant an almost exclusively Protestant Christianity, for Roman Catholics remained a very small minority in the country during her lifetime, and they tended to keep a low social profile in English society and so did not mix very freely.[2] Among Protestant Christians in England, there were a number of nonconformists or dissenters, Quakers, Baptists, and others, who disagreed with the Church of England for a whole host of reasons, but there were few dissenters among the gentry, the circle in which the Austens mixed socially. For them, *religious* would have been synonymous with the beliefs and rituals of practising Anglicans belonging to the Church of England. The eighteenth-century Anglicanism into which Jane was born was a faith that was tolerant and pragmatic, focusing on self-improvement and right behaviour, with a belief in change that comes not so much from miracles but through self-reflection and inner growth.

The word *spirituality* derives, as do *spirit* and *spiritual*, from the old French word *esprit*, which comes from the Latin *spiritus*, meaning, variously, "soul", "courage", "vigour", and "breath". It is related to the Latin verb *spirare*, meaning "to breathe". Just as breathing is an intrinsic part of human life, for many people spirituality is a dynamic and intrinsic aspect of their humanity. There are many definitions and understandings of spirituality. When these are all held together, three important themes emerge. Firstly, spirituality recognizes the importance of the deepest values by which people seek to live. Secondly, spirituality indicates the sense of a desire to live in the light of a realm that is beyond the material – one that some would call sacred. Thirdly, spirituality stresses the importance of an inner path enabling a person to discover the essence of his or her inner being. As we explore the life and writings of Jane Austen, we will consider these three themes: values and the importance they hold; what impression there is of looking beyond the material world; and the place of an inner path in exploring one's inner being.

This book is an attempt to explore and make suggestions about the ways in which Jane Austen thought about and acted upon the spiritual. This will be done through reflecting on what we know of her own life and character in the context of her times, on what has been revealed by the memories of her family, on what we can learn from the letters and prayers she left behind, and on what we can uncover in the storylines and characters of her novels. Approaching Jane Austen's wonderfully rich novels through the lens of spirituality is only one way of reading them – there are many other lenses. But reading *Sense and Sensibility*, *Pride and Prejudice*, *Northanger Abbey*, *Mansfield Park*, *Emma*, *Persuasion*, her writings from her youth, and her unfinished novels in this way can bring many fresh insights into her stories and characters, insights that can both bring further delight to our reading of her works and give inspiration to our own lives.

CHAPTER ONE

EARLY INFLUENCES, 1775–86

"… everything was soon happily over…" wrote the Reverend George Austen to his sister-in-law about the birth of Jane, his second daughter and seventh child. He described her as "… a present plaything for her sister Cassy and a future companion. She is to be Jenny…"[1]

Family

The warm use of pet names by their father for his two girls suggests that Jane was born into a loving family, where girls were as welcomed and loved as boys. It was a large and lively home. Jane had six older siblings. Her only sister, Cassandra, was nearly three when she was born and there were already five brothers: James, who was ten, George, nine, Edward, eight, Henry, four, and Frank, whom she followed, was one and a half. A last brother, Charles, was to follow Jane four years later. Unusually, in this age of frequent child deaths, all eight of the children survived into adulthood – and Jane was the first to die, at the age of forty-one. There were other children in the house as well, for her parents ran a small school, and a number of boys slept in the rectory attics and were taught by Revd Austen, alongside his own sons. The Austens ran the school as a large family rather than as an institution, and the schoolboys were like extra brothers to the Austen children.

Jane was born on 16 December in the depths of the harsh winter of 1775 in the small village of Steventon in Hampshire, seven miles west of the market town of Basingstoke. She was baptized at home, almost as soon as she was born, by her clergyman father, and it is likely that her first outing was up the road to her father's church for her public baptism at the beginning of the following April. For her first few months Jane was breastfed by her mother, but she was then put in the charge of a nurse or foster mother in the village, where she lived for another year, returning to live at home at the age of about one and a half. From a twenty-first-century perspective, with our modern understanding of the importance of child–parent bonding, this might seem a cruel practice, and much has been made by some of her biographers of the effect this could have had on Jane in the future,[2] but at that time this was a fairly common practice among people of the Austens' social class. Unlike many such children, who were sent far away, Jane stayed nearby in the village, was regularly visited by her parents and siblings, and was often brought home for a few hours.

One of her siblings, however, appears not to have lived at home, though he came on frequent visits. This was George, Jane's second oldest brother, who was nine when she was born. George suffered fits and failed to develop normally. It is possible that he was also deaf, as we know that Jane was able to communicate using some form of sign language[3] and she may have learned this through communicating with George. Throughout his life, he was cared for elsewhere. There are very few mentions of George in the family's letters and paperwork and, in the context of our time, which places a strong emphasis on social inclusion, this can seem uncaring. The Austen household was a large, boisterous one, so George was perhaps better protected and cared for elsewhere in a hopefully quieter environment. He died of dropsy at the age of seventy-two, a very good age in those days. He was then living in the village of Monks Sherborne, very close to the village where his oldest brother James was serving as vicar, and is described on his death certificate as having the position of "gentleman" at the time of his death. These facts suggest that he may have been well cared for and treated respectfully throughout his life.

Revd Austen's early description of Jane as "a present plaything" and a "future companion" for her sister Cassandra was to prove prophetic, for Jane and Cassandra were to be lifelong companions, always sharing a home except when one or the other was away visiting family or friends. It was said of Jane as a child that if Cassandra's head were to be cut off, Jane would have had hers cut off too.[4] Such a close bond between Jane and her sister may have inspired the very deep closeness of sisters Elinor and Marianne in *Sense and Sensibility* and Jane and Elizabeth in *Pride and Prejudice*.

Money was a pressing concern for Jane's parents, neither of whom had any inherited income, and we know that at the time of Jane's birth her father was fairly heavily in debt to various relations. Parish clergy were paid by tithes, which was a tax on the produce of the village land, payable by law to the rector of the parish. The tithes from Revd George Austen's parishes brought in only £210 a year, which would have been inadequate for the needs of his growing family. So George Austen needed to look beyond his parish work for his income. As well as running a school within his home, he farmed some nearby land, whose produce further supplemented his income. Jane would have grown up without illusions about the reality of living on a tight budget, even though she had links into the aristocratic world through her mother's family and her father's connections.

Cassandra Leigh, Jane's mother, was proud of the Leigh family's social position and links with the aristocracy, for her family was descended from a Lord Mayor of London, Sir Thomas Leigh, who in 1558 had proclaimed Elizabeth I queen. Cassandra's paternal grandfather was a squire of Adlestrop in

Gloucestershire who had married the sister of a duke, James Brydges, first Duke of Chandos. But Cassandra Leigh was the daughter of a third son, and so no fortune had come her way. Her father, Revd Thomas Leigh, was the rector of Harpsden in Oxfordshire. Cassandra had lived there until she moved with her parents to Bath, where her father died in 1764.

George Austen, Jane's father, did not have such aristocratic connections, and his life had had an unpromising start. He was born in Tonbridge in Kent and his mother died when he was just a year old. His father, William Austen, who was a surgeon, remarried but died when George was six. His stepmother took no further interest in George and his two sisters. William's will appointed two paternal uncles, Francis and Stephen, as guardians to the three children. As Francis was a bachelor, the children initially lived with Stephen, who had a young family, but he treated them with harshness and neglect.[5] Fortunately, Francis, who was a successful solicitor in Sevenoaks, had a greater concern for George, who soon came back to Tonbridge to live with an aunt, and at the age of ten began his formal education at Tonbridge School. Hard-working and bright, he won a fellowship to Oxford, and later an exhibition made it possible for him to take a Master's degree. He was ordained and held various roles: as a curate in Kent, a master at his old school, and a fellow at Oxford University.

It was through the wealthy husband of one of his second cousins, Thomas Knight, who was patron of the living of Steventon (which meant he had inherited the right to appoint clergy to that parish), that George was made rector there. His uncle Francis soon added in the neighbouring parish of Deane, where he was the patron. We learn much of the power and potential influence of a patron over a poor clergyman in the depiction of the relationship between Lady Catherine de Bourgh and Mr Collins in *Pride and Prejudice*. George Austen, however, was more fortunate than Mr Collins, for his patrons did not expect him to exhibit the sort of fawning behaviour Mr Collins showed to his patron.[6] In 1764, George married Cassandra Leigh in Bath, soon after her father's death. He and Cassandra may well have met in Oxford, as she had an uncle who was Master of Balliol College.

All of Jane's parents' social connections gave the family a prominent position in the area. George's Steventon patron, Thomas Knight, was a wealthy local landowner, owning an estate at nearby Chawton and land in and around Steventon, though he mainly lived on his estate at Godmersham in Kent. As a relation of their community's landowner, George would have been seen very much as his representative in the area and would have been required to act as "squire" in Thomas Knight's absence. Jane's mother's aristocratic and academic family connections enabled the family to move in the best social circles, and George's own educational and academic background would have ensured that he was highly respected. As a consequence, Jane's family received invitations for balls, parties, and other social occasions from all of the leading local families.

In spite of his education and potential, George Austen seemed content with his relatively poor livings, and stayed in Steventon for forty years until he retired to Bath in 1801. He does not appear to have sought a more prestigious parish despite all his social connections and academic attainments. In later life, Henry recalled his father as having been "not only a profound scholar, but professing a most exquisite taste in every species of literature".[7] He was also a gentle, kind, and indulgent father. After his death Jane wrote to her brother Frank of the "virtuous & happy life"[8] of their "Excellent Father"[9] and remarked, "... his tenderness as a Father, who can do justice to?"[10]

Jane's mother was a good manager of the home and family, being down to earth and practical. Known for her intelligent wit and sense of humour, she had also grown up in a lively home where she had entertained her family and visitors with her poetry and charades. She could be sharp and was not backward in recognizing the foibles of others, so it is likely that Jane inherited much of her wit and her acerbic eye from her mother.

Village Life and Society

The village of Steventon, where Jane Austen grew up, was to be reflected in the conservative communities within most of her six main novels, and was the world in which she felt happiest and most secure. Just like Highbury in *Emma*, Steventon was a village community where each inhabitant knew, and was known by, their social rank, and related to other people accordingly. Despite her family's financial concerns, Jane was born into a position of social privilege. Through her father's position as their clergyman, she would have known all the families in the village – and that knowledge would have been greater of those who worked on the family's farm or as domestic staff in their home. She would have visited poorer families when there was sickness or need. However, as regards class, the family were on a social par only with the Digweed family at Steventon Manor: the only people from the immediate parish whom the Austens could have met as equals on social occasions. The term "neighbourhood", so often used in Jane Austen's novels, referred to those families within easy travelling distance, who could meet each other for a visit during the day or for an evening's entertainment. The neighbourhood of the Austens, therefore, would have covered a wider area than the immediate parishes of Steventon and Deane. As members of the gentry, the Austens would technically have been below people who ranked as aristocracy, but because both of her parents had aristocratic connections, they could mix socially with a wider group of people than would otherwise have been expected. Their neighbourhood was made up of the families of clergymen, squires, aristocrats, members of parliament, doctors, and lawyers, whose homes and social occasions were open to them – all living within a range of about fifteen miles of Steventon.[11]

For the aristocratic Mr Darcy and the land-owning Bingleys of *Pride and Prejudice*, the neighbourhood around the small town of Meryton would be smaller than it was for the socially inferior Bennet family. Mrs Bennet, who could socialize with a wide group of people, cannot see this, which leads to embarrassment for her more perceptive daughter Elizabeth during a conversation between the families. Darcy commented, "In a country neighbourhood you move in a very confined and unvarying society," but Mrs Bennet insists, "I believe there are few neighbourhoods larger. I know we dine with four and twenty families."

As the popularity of Jane Austen's work grew in the later part of her life, she was once asked to broaden the range and scope of her novels. But she was determined to continue writing of the world with which she was familiar: "Three or four families in a country village is the very thing to work on,"[12] she wrote to her niece Anna. As well as the society she found in villages, Jane loved the countryside, and she gave some of her favourite characters, Elizabeth Bennet, Fanny Price, and Anne Elliot, her own love of walking through country lanes, enjoying the change of the seasons and watching the night skies. There is no doubt that the rural context of Jane's childhood and youth was a supremely important influence on her development.

Education and Schools

Education was highly prized by Jane's family. Stories would no doubt have passed down to Jane of her paternal great-grandmother Elizabeth Austen, who had been left badly off following the death of her husband, with six sons and a daughter to educate. Despite the drop in social status that such a step involved, she took up a post as matron and housekeeper at Sevenoaks School in 1708, in return for the free schooling of her sons. She passed down to her grandson Revd George, and thus to her great-granddaughter Jane Austen, the belief that intelligence and eloquence count for more in life than an inherited fortune.

There is every evidence that George Austen sought to develop such intelligence and eloquence in his children and pupils. He took on the education at home of all of his sons (except George, who, as we have seen, lived elsewhere), before they moved out into the world. That his sons took up such different careers is indicative that he helped them to find the paths in life that suited their natural abilities and dispositions.

James, the oldest, was known in the family as "the scholar". His mother wrote of him: "Classical Knowledge, Literary Taste, and the power of Eloquent Composition he possessed to the highest degree..."[13] He went to Oxford at just fourteen, obtaining a scholarship as "founder's kin" through his mother's connections. In her childhood, Jane's reading was very much directed by James, who clearly took a keen interest in his little sister's prowess in reading and writing.

Edward, as a twelve-year-old boy, caught the attention of the distant cousin and patron of Revd George, the aristocratic Thomas Knight of Godmersham, who requested that Edward should spend increasing periods of time in Kent with him and his wife, Catherine. As it became clear that they would have no children of their own to inherit their properties, the Knights expressed a wish to adopt Edward when he was sixteen, their only condition being that he change his surname from Austen to Knight. Thomas then continued Edward's education by training him up to be a country gentleman and, in time, to run the Knight family estates, which included the estate of Chawton in Hampshire. Much later in the Austen family story, Edward's role as squire of Chawton would play an indispensable part in Jane's vocation as a writer. Edward's relationship with his family appears to have remained warm and loving despite the abrupt change in his social and financial status.

Henry, described by his father as the most talented of Jane's brothers, followed James to Oxford when he was fifteen. Henry was less steady and serious than James, and though he was to become in time Jane's favourite brother, her reaction to one of his escapades – "Oh, what a Henry!"[14] – shows that she was never under any illusions about his foibles. This is how, in later years, his niece Anna remembered him:

> ... *the handsomest of the family, and in the opinion of his own father, the most talented. There were others who formed a different estimate, but for the most part, he was greatly admired. Brilliant in conversation he was, and like his father, blessed with a hopefulness of temper which, in adapting itself to all circumstances, even the most adverse, served to create a perpetual sunshine.*[15]

Frank was known for his energetic liveliness – he was running about before he was fourteen months old. He loved the outdoor life and, by the age of seven, had bought his own pony and joined the local hunt. Just before his twelfth birthday, he went to the Royal Naval Academy at Portsmouth, becoming the first of the Austen sons to go to sea. His father's wisdom in permitting Frank's career choice was truly justified, for Frank rose steadily through the naval ranks, eventually becoming Admiral of the Fleet. Charles, the youngest, followed Frank into the Navy – and he too was clearly well suited to the life, as in time he was made a Rear-Admiral. Jane followed the careers of her naval brothers with great interest, and there is no doubt that much from these brothers' experiences and adventures found its way into the pages of *Mansfield Park* and *Persuasion*.

With so many boys around in her childhood, the question must surely be asked whether there is something of Jane herself in her description of Catherine Morland of *Northanger Abbey*, who was fond of "all boy's play", had a love of dirt and running about the country, and spent hours rolling down a grassy slope in the rectory garden. There was such a grassy slope in the Steventon Rectory garden, but given that we know Jane was writing seriously by the age of twelve, we can be confident that her love of reading began long before that of Catherine, who didn't begin to appreciate books until she was fifteen.

In another way, Jane's childhood was not to be the same as Catherine's for, when they were ten and seven, Cassandra and Jane went away to school. The reasons for Jane's going away to school at such a young age are not clear. It may be that her parents spotted how bright she was and knew they could not give her the time, attention, and formal education that they recognized she needed. It may be that they needed the girls' bedroom to fit in more boys for their own school. For Jane to learn alongside the boys would not have been seen as acceptable, though it is likely that she had already picked up a lot of learning informally. A later reason given by the family is that Jane hated being parted from her sister, for where Cassandra went, there Jane always wanted to go too.

It appears that the idea of the girls going away to school arose when Mrs Austen's sister, Mrs Cooper, appealed to the Austens to send Cassandra to be a companion to her daughter, Jane Cooper, who was going to a school in Oxford. This establishment was being set up by her husband's widowed sister, Mrs Cawley. There is little that we can learn about Jane Austen's experience here from her letters and novels. None of her childhood letters survive, if they ever existed. Her *Juvenilia* (youthful writings) make no reference to schools or children. However, in a letter written when she was thirty-two, Jane declared that she had been a very shy child,[16] which would fit with such an emotional dependence on her older sister and could have led to her insistence that she could not be parted from Cassandra. In her novel *Mansfield Park* we have a painful account of the shy Fanny, sent away from home when she was nine, suffering agonies in her homesickness and timidity, which may reflect Jane's own experiences. Fanny, however, unlike Jane, leaves home completely on her own and so is separated from her favourite sibling, her older brother William.

The school in Oxford attended by Jane and Cassandra would probably have been set up within Mrs Cawley's home, like their own parents' school at Steventon Rectory. Jane would have had lessons in handwriting, languages, dancing, and sewing. The school soon moved to Southampton, where all three girls became ill with an infectious fever, possibly typhus fever, which was rife in the city at the time. It had been brought there by troops returning from Gibraltar, for the war with France and the American War of Independence meant that there was great military activity in the area. A letter from Jane Cooper alerted the Austen parents and the girls were brought home just six months after they had started – Jane Austen being particularly poorly. All three girls survived, though the infection was passed on to Mrs Cooper, who died.

After a year at home the three girls were sent off to school again, this time to a much more well-established venture, the Abbey School in Reading, where they stayed for three years. It is not known why their parents decided to bring Jane and Cassandra home from here, but possibly they felt that the girls were not learning enough to justify the annual fees of over thirty-five pounds.[17] Jane's experience seems not to have given her a high view of schools for girls: "I would rather be a Teacher at a school (and I can think of nothing worse) than marry a Man I did not like" are words she puts into the mouth of Emma, the leading character in *The Watsons*, and she once wrote in a letter to Cassandra "... to be rational in anything is great praise, especially in the ignorant class of school mistresses..."[18]

We can be in no doubt that Jane picked up a huge amount of learning through her own reading and her interaction with her family. From the earliest age, at church and at home, she would have heard the Bible read aloud. This would have been the King James Version, and it would have had a strong influence on her spirituality. Much of the Bible is made up of stories, in which good usually ultimately triumphs over evil. In the Old Testament she would have heard stories of the prophets – those who see and proclaim what others do not see, and suffer as a result, but are eventually vindicated and rewarded. She would have come across, in both Testaments, the idea of death and resurrection – not just in the life of Jesus Christ, but in the lives of other characters who suffered and were transformed by that suffering. There are villains as well as good people in the Bible stories, however – not everyone is prepared to accept that they need transformation, not everyone changes, and not everyone receives a reward. We will see these biblical themes and stories reflected in Jane's novels.

Two of her childhood books survive. *Goody Two-Shoes*, an anonymous variation of the Cinderella story, was published in 1765. The story popularized the phrase "goody two-shoes", often used to describe an excessively virtuous person. The fable tells of Goody Two-Shoes, the nickname of a poor orphan girl named Margery Meanwell, who goes through life with only one shoe. When a rich gentleman gives her a complete pair, she is so happy that she tells everyone she has "two shoes". Later, Margery becomes a teacher and marries a rich widower.

This gaining of wealth shows that her virtuousness has been rewarded, a popular theme in the children's literature of the era. Jane's second childhood book was La Fontaine's *Faibles Choisies*, a book of French fables, some by Aesop, which was also regarded at the time as providing an excellent education in morals.

At a precociously young age, however, Jane also began to read books written for adults. At a time when there was a belief in some quarters that reading could be harmful to the appropriate development of girls, she had uncensored access to her father's library of over five hundred volumes, and she was soon reading widely. Unlike the later Victorian era, when society became more prudish and rigid, especially for women, these were generally more liberal times and many people of all classes in England had the leisure and inclination to read whatever they wished. The German author Karl Philipp Moritz wrote in his *Travels in England* in 1782, when Jane was seven, of his surprise at how many people in England read:

> *Certain it is that the English classical authors are read more generally, beyond all comparison, than the German; which in general are read only by the learned; or, at most, by the middle class of people. The English national authors are in all hands, and read by all people, of which the innumerable editions they have gone through are a sufficient proof. My landlady, who is only a tailor's widow, reads her Milton; and tells me, that her late husband first fell in love with her on this very account: because she read Milton with such proper emphasis. This single instance, perhaps, would prove but little; but I have conversed with several people of the lower class, who all knew their national authors, and who all have read many, if not all, of them.*[19]

As well as novels, poetry was written and passed round to family and friends, with Mrs Austen and James being particularly keen poetry writers. In the evenings the family gathered to hear books and poetry read aloud, from both published sources and their own writings. Under the leadership of the oldest brother, James, plays were put on in the family barn, with local families invited to be actors and audience, and with Jane participating with great enthusiasm. The fact that she was later to dedicate many of her teenage pieces of writing, her *Juvenilia*, to members of her immediate family suggests that they encouraged and nurtured her youthful literary development.

One touching proof of Revd George Austen's indulgence of his younger daughter's childish imagination can be found in the Steventon Church marriage register, which contains records of all the weddings held there between 1755 and 1812. At the front of the book where there are specimen entries to show clergy how to complete the records, some of these have been altered by a youthful Jane Austen. She created a banns entry for "Henry Frederic Howard Fitzwilliam and Jane Austen", a marriage entry for "Edmund Arthur William Mortimer of Liverpool and Jane Austen", and a later marriage entry for plain "Jack Smith and Jane Smith late Austen".

Church and Faith

As we have seen, Jane Austen was born into a family that abounded in clergy of the Church of England. As well as there being many clergy in her parents' and grandparents' generations, her oldest brother James was ordained when she was only twelve, and another brother, Henry, would be ordained the year before she died. She writes of clergy in her novels with great ease because she mixed naturally with them from her earliest days, and she knew and instinctively understood the world of a village rector and the role of the church in a village community.

Though Revd George Austen struggled to make ends meet for his large family, through the eighteenth century the value of tithes and glebe land had generally increased, making clergy better off and enabling many of them to rise in social status. This meant that country gentlemen who had the patronage of a church in their gift came more and more to regard these livings as appropriate career choices for their younger sons. This is the case at the end of *Mansfield Park*, where Edmund is installed as the Mansfield vicar, living just a short walk away from his father's house. As the social status of many clergy grew higher, expectations for the amenities of their homes increased. At the end of *Sense and Sensibility*, work needs to be done to Delaford Parsonage to make it a suitable home for Colonel Brandon's brother-in-law – new wallpaper, shrubberies, and a curved carriage driveway leading up to the house are all being planned.

Readers of Jane Austen's novels will be very aware of the leisured existence of the clergy that she depicts – they seem to have had endless time for the country pursuits of hunting and shooting, and for visiting and social evenings in the neighbourhood. Jane's father had much time aside from his parish duties to devote to his family, his school, and his farming, as well as to parties, balls, and gatherings with the local gentry. There were a few reasons for this. Firstly, at the beginning of the nineteenth century, four-fifths of the population lived, like the Austens, in villages or hamlets, and the vast majority of clergy lived in parishes of fewer than five hundred parishioners. In the Austens' time, Steventon Parish had thirty families, and Deane was smaller still. The combined population of the two parishes scarcely amounted to three hundred people.[20] Secondly, there was little pressure exerted by bishops or by public opinion to compel a clergyman to do more than he wished. On Sundays he would be expected to "read prayers" twice: that is, to follow the liturgy of the Book of Common Prayer Morning and Evening

Services, usually at 10 a.m. and 3 p.m. There would be an occasional Holy Communion service following Morning Prayer. A sermon was expected at one of these services, but there was no requirement that it would be an original one, written for that Sunday, as it was perfectly proper to read one from one of the many books published for the purpose. We know from her letters that Jane frequently read such books of sermons, often with great interest. In between Morning and Evening Prayer there could be some extra services – baptisms, weddings, burials, or the churching of women after childbirth. During the week, clergy were not expected to say the daily offices of Morning and Evening Prayer in their churches, and midweek services were rare. There would be some sick visiting to do, but again expectations were low: Mr Elton of *Emma* is highly thought of in Highbury for the amount of sick visiting he carries out. There would be an occasional parish meeting – it was such a meeting that caused Henry Tilney on one occasion to prolong his stay in his parish at Woodston, preventing him from returning to Northanger Abbey after he had taken his Sunday services.

Many clergy held the livings of more than one parish, and this was referred to as "plurality". Usually a rector would employ a curate, who was often paid very poorly, to conduct the duties in any parish where the rector was not resident, and in all the parishes when he was away. Though there was disapproval of this practice, little was done to make any changes. When he took on Deane as a second parish to Steventon, Revd Austen did make it clear to the Bishop of Winchester that the churches were only two miles apart and he would be able to conduct a service in each of the two churches on Sundays.

From a very young age, Jane would have attended services at church and at home, taking part in the responses as soon as she could remember them, and listening to the Bible readings and to her father's sermons and prayers. In church, her father wore a black cassock and white surplice – there were no colourful vestments, altar frontals, flowers, or candles. There would be very few coloured stained-glass windows – some remained from medieval times but most stained-glass windows in English parish churches were put in by the Victorians. In parishes like Steventon that had not been influenced by the evangelical movement, there would be no hymn singing. Only cathedrals and some larger churches had choirs singing the psalms and canticles; in Steventon, the psalms would be said or sung to a metrical chant. This was all part of Jane Austen's expectations, and no hymn or psalm tunes were found in her collection of music after her death. While such unadorned church worship might seem outwardly very plain and dull to us, it was the traditional Anglican worship of the time.[21]

Jane's father, along with the other local clergy in the area and most of the clergy in her family, had studied at Oxford. There the theology syllabus, which had remained unchanged for decades, had its focus on "natural theology", emphasizing how we learn about God through our own human reason, focusing on the evidence of God in the design of the created world. Jane Austen's religious upbringing was within traditional eighteenth-century Anglicanism, and was the antithesis of some of the popular religiosity of the turbulent previous century, which had seen the beheading of the Catholic King Charles I, followed by the rule of the puritan Oliver Cromwell. Religious "enthusiasm" of all sorts was regarded with suspicion, for it was seen as having killed a king. Thus the measured and broad Anglican Church that evolved, which still very much held sway in Steventon in Jane's childhood years, stressed order, balance, and duty.

Those who had particular religious influence at the time, and whose writings no doubt made up part of Revd George Austen's library, included the philosopher John Locke, the so-called "Father of the Enlightenment" (1632–1704), who stressed tolerance, the need for a balance between reason and revelation, and the responsibility of each person as a moral being before God. Another voice was that of Archbishop John Tillotson (1630–94). In his popular and widely read sermons, he stressed the need for a Christianity that was lived out in everyday life; as did Bishop Joseph Butler (1692–1752), who emphasized the importance of balance between the internal and external components of Christianity – the holding together of what is believed and what is lived out. Together, such teaching reinforced the importance of a Christian faith which made sense to people's minds, was practised without excess of showy religious devotion, respected people's consciences rather than being overly intrusive, upheld the structures of society, and expected that people would recognize their moral duty to their neighbours in a way that was appropriate to their place in society.

Such faith, for an individual, led to the quiet belief that we see developing in Fanny Price in *Mansfield Park*, as she seeks to obey her conscience and to develop the virtues that would enable her to play out her duty fully in the family and society. The role of the local church was to encourage communities where bonds were governed by duty and loyalty: by manor house and church, squire and clergyman side by side, as we see in the partnership between the squire, Sir Thomas Bertram, and the clergyman, Edmund Bertram, supported by his wife, Fanny, in the closing chapter of *Mansfield Park*. Both parties would uphold the law of the land and the duties of the church, both endeavouring to give the right example for all in their charge to follow.

We hear Revd George Austen's own words of advice in a long letter written in 1788 to Jane's fourteen-year-old brother Frank, as he was preparing to leave the Royal Naval Academy and go on his first sea voyage. Revd Austen entitles his letter "Memorandum for the use of Mr F W Austen on his going to the East Indies on board his Majesty's ship *Perseverance* (Captain Smith)". This letter shows George Austen's belief that his son would continue in the conscientiousness that he had always demonstrated to his family:

Your conduct, as it respects yourself, chiefly comprehends sobriety and prudence. The former you know the importance of to your health, your morals and your fortune. I shall therefore say nothing more to enforce the observance of it. I thank God you have not at present the least disposition to deviate from it. Prudence extends to a variety of objects. Never any action of your life in which it will not be your interest to consider what she directs! She will teach you the proper disposal of your time and the careful management of your money, – two very important trusts for which you are accountable. [22]

At his death, this letter was found among Frank's most treasured possessions, frayed from being constantly taken out and reread. Frank had risen through the Navy to become Admiral of the Fleet in 1863, and yet he had remained well loved and respected by all ranks on his ships, and was affectionately known as "the officer who knelt in church". As we have seen from the letters that she would later send him when their father died, Jane shared Frank's high estimation of their father, prizing his tenderness and the exemplary way he led his life. Looking at the advice George Austen gave his son, it is clear that morality – doing the right thing, based on right principles – was immensely important to him. And it would have been equally important that such principles were lived out in the lives of all his children, including Jane.

With the exception of her experiences away at school, which may not have been good, Jane had a happy and secure childhood, part of a close family, in a home, church, and community where she was loved and encouraged to play her full part. The importance of the themes of home, church, and community to her, throughout her life, can be traced back to these early years, for from them she gained the seeds of her own spiritual growth, and learned the values of respect, duty, and self-discipline. Through her wide reading she gained an understanding of worlds other than her own, and from the Bible and through her father's sermons she would have learned about the Christian understanding of Kingdom of God – the reign of the justice, peace, and love of God, which was to be lived out by Christians through moral conduct in this world and anticipated in the world to come. She was brought up to hold implicitly Christian beliefs that reflected the traditional Anglicanism of her time, with the emphasis on the inner meaning of faith rather than on an outer show of religiosity. Jane, like each of her brothers, was encouraged to find and develop her own path in life through the discovery of her own particular interests and talents, to explore the world through wide reading, and to think for herself – all seeds for the rich inner life she was to develop as she grew older. The enormous encouragement that she received from her family, and especially from her father, to think for herself, to read and to write, cannot be underestimated. All these early encouragements were hugely important influences on Jane Austen's development, both as a writer and as a woman of faith.

CHAPTER TWO

THE DEVELOPMENT OF THE WRITER, 1787–1800

After returning from school in Reading, and apart from visits to family or friends, Jane was to remain at home for the rest of her life, although that home would change location. Until she was twenty-five, home was the Steventon Rectory. One by one her brothers left: James and Henry to study in Oxford; Edward to live with his adopted family in Kent; Frank and Charles to join the Navy. For Jane and Cassandra, outwardly at least, there were no opportunities for adventure, but these were crucial years for Jane in shaping the writer that she was to become. In the next chapter, we will turn our attention to her first novels, which she began in 1795 with *Elinor and Marianne*, a first draft of the work that would eventually become *Sense and Sensibility*. But first we will consider the other pieces of her writing from these Steventon years, and look at how events in her wider family and the world, during the closing years of the eighteenth and opening year of the nineteenth century, influenced her novel writing and her own spiritual development.

Reading Novels

Jane Austen once described her family as being "great novel-readers and not ashamed of being so..."[1] From her earliest days, she was used to hearing a wide variety of novels being read aloud and discussed by her family as they gathered together in the evenings. Jane read many essays and much poetry and followed her father in being an ardent admirer of the versatile writer and literary critic Samuel Johnson, and of the poetry of William Cowper. Many of Cowper's poems focused on everyday life and scenes of the countryside, a new departure for poetry in the eighteenth century – a focus that Jane was to reflect in her novels. She once described her family as being "great novel-readers and not ashamed of being so..." They were part of one of the many local lending libraries that had sprung up all over the country, giving her access to new novels as they were published, as well as the classics. The famous names of eighteenth-century fiction would all have been part of her reading: Fanny Burney, Daniel Defoe, Samuel Richardson, Henry Fielding, and Laurence Sterne. As we have seen, her reading was not censored in any way, so throughout her teenage years she read and reread the rather risqué contents of Henry Fielding's *The History of Tom Jones, a Foundling* and Laurence Sterne's *Tristram Shandy*. Her declared favourite novel, however, was Samuel Richardson's *The History of Sir Charles Grandison*, which he set out to write in response to Fielding's *Tom Jones*, with Sir Charles deliberately designed by the author to be a morally better hero.

Two particular literary genres were very popular during Jane's teenage years, the Gothic novel and the Romantic Sentimental novel. Gothic novels, which combined horror, death, and romance, were often set in the ruins of medieval castles or abbeys and were written to inculcate a pleasing sense of terror in the reader. The emergence of this genre can be traced to Horace Walpole's 1764 novel *The Castle of Otranto*, which is set in an ancient castle, housing ghosts, portraits that come to life, statues that drip blood, and trapdoors that lead to a bewildering maze of underground passages where a heroine is chased by terrifying figures. We can assume that the list of Gothic novels (some with blood-curdling titles) that Jane put into the mouth of Isabella Thorpe in *Northanger Abbey* were books with which she was familiar: *The Castle of Wolfenbach, Clermont, The Mysterious Warning, The Necromancer; or The Tale of the Black Forest, The Midnight Bell, The Orphan of the Rhine*, and *Horrid Mysteries*.

The Romantic Sentimental novel, another eighteenth-century literary genre, sought to evoke an emotional response from its readers. These stories feature scenes of distress and tenderness, with the plots centring more on the main characters' emotions and responses to situations than on action. An early example of such a novel was Samuel Richardson's *Pamela: or, Virtue Rewarded*. Its leading character, the fifteen-year-old maidservant Pamela Andrews, is subjected to repeated unwanted advances by the lecherous landowner Mr B. Her response is unequivocal: "I will bear any thing you can inflict upon me with Patience, even to the laying down of my Life, to shew my Obedience to you in other Cases; but I cannot be patient, I cannot be passive, when my Virtue is at Stake!" Finally her virtue and worth are recognized and honoured by Mr B, and he proposes an equitable marriage.

The *Juvenilia*

In 1787, Jane Austen began seriously to devote her spare time to writing. She left twenty-two pieces – plays, stories, and story fragments – written in her teenage years. We know these today as her *Juvenilia*. The first of these was written when she was twelve years old, and the last when she was about seventeen. These writings were clearly very important to her in later life, as she carefully copied them into three notebooks, to which she made additions and corrections as late as 1809, though never with any idea of their being read outside the family circle. Two of these notebooks were gifts from her father, and in one he has written on the inside front cover "Effusions of fancy by a young lady consisting of tales in a style entirely new". These stories enabled Jane to play her part in the Austen family evenings, when members of the family entertained each other by reading their writings aloud. Most of these pieces are dedicated to members of the family and no doubt contain many allusions to shared jokes and common favourite readings.[2] In them, we see the young Jane looking at the adult world with eyes wide open, amused at the intrigues, deceptions, and emotions that she has seen or read about. The stories are audacious and satirical parodies – her characters often drink too much, are violent, and engage in sexual misdemeanours. The thread throughout them all is a satirical take on the Romantic Sentimental novels, history books, and moral essays of her day. So we meet, among a host of memorable characters, the perfidious Lady Williams of Pammydiddle, the serial lover Sir William Mountague, and the splendid Charles Adams, a young man of "so dazzling a beauty that none but eagles could look him in the Face". These characters and their adventures and misfortunes are delivered with a delightful sense of mischief:

> ... *During this happy state of Harmony, the eldest Miss Fitzroy ran off with the coachman and the amiable Rebecca was asked in marriage by Captain Roger of Buckinghamshire. Mrs Fitzroy did not approve of the match on account of the tender years of the young couple, Rebecca being but thirty-six and Captain Roger little more than sixty-three. To remedy this objection, it was agreed that they should wait a little while till they were a good deal older.*

So states Jane Austen in the first of these stories, *Frederic and Elfrida*, written when she was perhaps only twelve years old. In the first *Juvenilia* stories, she has a similar style to that of the nine-year-old Daisy Ashford whose famous story *The Young*

Visitors, written in 1891, also parodied what she as a child saw as she looked at the adult world. Though hailed as a child prodigy, Daisy, unlike Jane Austen, did not develop her talent sufficiently to achieve fame as an adult writer.

The *Juvenilia* show that Jane Austen was fascinated, from an early age, by the intrigues and speculations that swirl around a community with regard to the marriage prospects of the eligible bachelors in their midst – a subject she was to return to in her opening chapter of *Pride and Prejudice*: "It is a truth universally acknowledged, that a single man in possession of a good fortune, must be in want of a wife." We can imagine her listening in rapt attention to the gossip within her neighbourhood, and joyfully parodying what she heard. So she created this ending to the ninth and final chapter of her next work, *Jack and Alice*:

> *In the meantime, the inhabitants of Pammydiddle were in a state of the greatest astonishment and wonder, a report being circulated of the intended marriage of Charles Adams. The lady's name was still a secret. Mr and Mrs Jones imagined it to be Miss Johnson, but **she** knew better; all **her** fears were centred in his cook, when, to the astonishment of everyone, he was publicly united to Lady Williams.*

The emotionalism of characters within the genre of the Romantic Sentimental novel, which Jane Austen was later to explore further in the character of Marianne in *Sense and Sensibility*, is mocked in the final words of *Edgar and Emma*:

> *It was with difficulty that Emma could refrain from tears on hearing of the absence of Edgar; she remained, however, tolerably composed till the Willmots were gone, when, having no check to the overflowings of her grief, she gave free vent to them, and retiring to her own room, continued in tears the remainder of her life.*

And in "A Letter from a Young Lady, whose feelings being too Strong for her Judgement led her into the commission of Errors which her Heart disapproved", we see her imagining a storyline way beyond the reality of the life she had witnessed in and around her father's country parishes. Anna Parker writes to her confidante Ellinor:

> *I murdered my father at a very early period of my life, I have since murdered my mother and am now going to murder my sister. I have changed my religion so often that at present I have no idea of any left, I have been a perjured witness in every trial for this past 12 months… and I have forged my own will. In short there is scarcely a crime that I have not committed – but I am now going to reform.*

The reformation was clearly short-lived!

Jane Austen's *Juvenilia* were just that – immature. When Richard III's body was discovered in a car park in Leicester, a visitor centre was opened nearby in 2015. An information board in the centre quotes part of Jane Austen's *The History of England* in support of Richard's good qualities: "The character of this Prince has been in general very severely treated by historians, but as he was *York*, I am rather inclined to dispose him a very respectable man." The interpretation board correctly informs the visitor that these words were written by Jane Austen in 1791, but neglects to say that she was only fifteen years old at the time. Nor does it mention that she described herself on the title page of this work as "a partial, prejudiced and ignorant Historian", or that the "history" was consciously written as a parody of her school history textbook, written by Oliver Goldsmith. Perhaps it is because these youthful, humorous writings are so little known that the facts have not been made clear.

In her longest work *Love and Freindship* (*sic*), we see shadows of some of her more mature characters, for, with its critique of sensibility, it resembles *Sense and Sensibility*. Laura is not a parody but is usually quite rational, giving us for the first time in Jane Austen's writings a heroine who looks at the other characters critically. It is an epistolary novel – a popular format in the eighteenth century, meaning one written as a series of letters. In this story, all the letters are written by Laura, and in her last letter she says:

> *When we arrived at Edinburgh, Sir Edward told me that, as the widow of his son, he desired I would accept from his hands the sum of four hundred a year. I graciously promised that I would, but could not help observing that the unsympathetic baronet offered it more on account of my being the widow of Edward than in being the refined and amiable Laura.*

Ultimately, however, Jane Austen assigns to Laura a future appropriate to the heroine of the Romantic Sentimental genre, for she concludes:

> *I took up my residence in a romantic village in the Highlands of Scotland, where I have ever since continued, and where I can, uninterrupted by unmeaning visits, indulge, in a melancholy solitude, my unceasing lamentations for the death of my father, my mother, my husband, and my friend.*

Another epistolary novel is *The Three Sisters*, but now the letters are written by two different characters, allowing Jane the chance to try out different voices who hold different perspectives on the same situation. The kernels of some of her characters in *Pride and Prejudice* emerge, and as well as the contrast of the different voices we can also perceive some gentle moral criticism. Jane was to use the epistolary framework for the first draft of *Sense and Sensibility*, which explores the very contrasting characters of the two sisters Elinor and Marianne. Unlike some of her predecessors, who are prone to faint, complain, or even drink their way through their problems, in *The Three Sisters* Catherine is a heroine who faces her difficulties by withdrawing to her bower, which "possessed such a charm over her senses as constantly to tranquillise her mind and quiet her spirits". Here we find a character who is beginning to explore her inner being, and in Kitty's bower we see perhaps a hint of the white room of Mansfield Park, which was to be such a place of solace and inner growth for Fanny Price.

The Loiterer

In 1789, Jane's brother James, then a student at Oxford, started to publish a weekly magazine, entitled *The Loiterer*, with his brother Henry as his assistant. It was to run to sixty editions, containing pieces on Oxford life, and other members of the family contributed to it. In the ninth issue, dated 28 March 1789, there is a three-paragraph letter, written in a style parodying that of the Romantic Sentimental novel, complaining about the paper's lack of feminine interest, especially the lack of sensational fiction. "Get a new set of correspondents from among the young of both sexes, but particularly ours," the writer advises the editors, and then perhaps she would no longer see *The Loiterer* as "the stupidest work" of its kind. It is signed "Sophia Sentiment" and has a tone so similar to many of Jane's *Juvenilia* that it is very possible that she wrote it – she would have been thirteen at the time. If so, this letter would have been the first piece of her writing that she saw published. But, as with the four novels published in her lifetime, if this is her authorship, it remained anonymous.

Lady Susan

When she was eighteen or nineteen, Jane Austen wrote a longer piece which is believed to be her first complete novel. At sixty pages in a modern paperback, it was the longest piece she had written, though still very much shorter than her later completed novels. She transcribed it in 1805 but does not seem to have pursued publication for it, or given it a title. It was first published by her nephew with the second edition of his memoir of Jane Austen in 1871 titled *Lady Susan* after the main character. It was also written as a series of letters and follows the machinations of a worldly-wise, materialistic widow, with at least one affair behind her already, who is seeking to make her fortune by marrying money herself, and arranging a loveless match for her daughter. She has chosen for her a wealthy simpleton, Sir James, who is himself pursuing a Miss Manwaring. There is much that is familiar in tone from Jane's *Juvenilia*.

In 2016 *Lady Susan* was brought to the world's attention when it came out as the Whit Stillman film *Love and Friendship*, rather confusingly named after one of Jane's other *Juvenilia* pieces, as we have seen. Viewers have been surprised to see such a character as the malicious Lady Susan take the lead, and critics have asked whether such an anti-heroine could actually be a Jane Austen creation.

Why did Jane Austen abandon the eighteenth-century burlesque comedy format in her later novels? Was she suppressing her natural style, or were literary fashions changing? Lady Susan is recognized and admired for her wit, intelligence, and charm – and, in those elements, she bears some resemblance to Elizabeth Bennet, Mary Crawford, and Emma Woodhouse. Affairs, adultery, and betrayals do appear in the later novels, but always off stage. Perhaps Jane Austen recognized that the story had problems. The weakness of the story is that Lady Susan is so strongly drawn, and has all the best lines, and so all the other characters seem dull by comparison. As a result there is no positive world to aspire to, in contrast with Lady Susan's materialistic and corrupt one. We know that the countryside-loving Jane Austen did not put her own values into Lady Susan, for she has her describe Churchill, the home of the Vernons with whom she is staying, as "that insupportable spot, a country village". She may have enjoyed writing in Lady Susan's voice, but she did not endorse her morality, and she ensured that Lady Susan gets her just deserts. At the end, her wickedness is recognized and exposed, the formerly downtrodden daughter wins her mother's intended, and it is Lady Susan who ends up married to the simpleton Sir James. Jane Austen concludes:

> *Whether Lady Susan was, or was not, happy in her second choice, I do not see how it can ever be ascertained, for who would take her assurance of it on either side of the question? The world must judge from probabilities; she had nothing against her but her husband and her conscience. Sir James may seem to have drawn a harder lot than mere folly merited. I leave him, therefore, to all the pity that anybody can give him.*

Jane Austen recognized that Lady Susan would not change, and that she had no capacity for the inner growth that the author was beginning to explore in the characters of some of her later *Juvenilia*. Later, in Mrs Norris of Mansfield Park, Jane would again depict a malicious woman, though one who lacks Lady Susan's wit, intelligence, and charm. Mrs Norris also gets her punishment in the end – but she is only a minor character. Jane Austen did not write another book like *Lady Susan*. After this story, her main characters were always to be women with the capacity to reflect, learn, and grow inwardly.

Letter Writing

Jane's early writings may also have included many letters. As Cassandra and Jane grew old enough to pay long visits to friends and family, they were often parted, and we know they wrote regularly to each other. But the first letter by Jane that we are aware of today was written in 1796, when she was twenty.

When we read Jane Austen's letters, we must note that she would not have expected that they would ever be read outside the family circle, and so care must be taken not to deduce too much hard fact and opinion from lines written to amuse her sister and practise her own wit. Most of the letters, particularly those to Cassandra, are made up of humdrum family news and village gossip. Jane Austen was very aware of issues concerning privacy and honour when it came to reading others' private correspondence, as we can see in *Persuasion*. Anne Elliot has just been shown a letter by Mrs Smith that was sent to her husband by William Elliot, in which he speaks very disrespectfully of Anne's father, Sir Walter Elliot:

> *She was obliged to recollect that her seeing the letter was a violation of the laws of honour, that no one ought to be judged or to be known by such testimonies, that no private correspondence could bear the eye of others, before she could recover calmness enough to return the letter which she had been meditating over…*

Some comments in Jane Austen's letters can be seen as malicious, such as her description of a Mrs Hall, who had just given birth to a dead baby, delivered several weeks early "owing to a fright. I suppose she happened unawares to look at her husband";[3] or of a domestic painter at the Castle in Southampton: "I suppose whenever the walls want no touching up, he is employed about my lady's face…"[4] We do not know the context of some of the comments in her letters, such as her words to Cassandra about General Sir John Moore, who had died at the Battle of Corunna in Spain: "I am sorry to find that Sir J. Moore has a mother living, but though a very heroic son he might not be a very necessary one to her happiness. Deacon Morrell may be more to Mrs. Morrell. I wish Sir John had united something of the Christian with the hero in his death."[5] Sir John's parents were neighbours of Jane's godfather, Revd Samuel Cooke, the vicar of Great Bookham in Surrey, so there was perhaps some private family knowledge or gossip. However, Jane's comments are often aimed as much at herself as at others, such as this one: "I do not like the Miss Blackstones; indeed I was always determined not to like them, so there is the less merit in it."[6]

In reading Jane Austen's letters, it is always important to note the recipient. About two-thirds of her extant letters are written to her sister, Cassandra, and they have a particular gossipy and satirical style. The others, mainly addressed to brothers, nieces, and friends, contain noticeably less ironic wit, and are often written to congratulate, commiserate, or – especially in the case of her nieces – comment on a particular piece of their writing. These letters are usually supportive and caring. We can assume that her relationship with her sister was so close that she did not feel the need to exhibit the "good manners" to Cassandra that were so important to her in her behaviour elsewhere. After a rare malicious comment to her brother Francis about a lady of their acquaintance, whom she describes as a woman who "likes her spasms and nervousness and the consequences they give her, better than anything else", she does then acknowledge that "[t]his is an ill-natured sentiment to send all over the Baltic!"[7]

Jane and Cassandra, though writing principally to pass on news, clearly also gave great entertainment to each other in their manner of writing. Jane says to Cassandra: "You must read your letters over *five* times in future before you send them, and then, perhaps, you may find them as entertaining as I do,"[8] and of her own letter writing: "I will endeavour to make this letter more worthy of your acceptance than my last, which was so shabby a one that I think Mr. Marshall could never charge you with the postage."[9] As with her *Juvenilia*, her letters gave her the opportunity to try out different styles of writing and turns of phrase; but also, particularly in letters to Cassandra, simply to write honestly and amusingly.

Visits to Family and Friends

As well as providing the opportunity to write letters, Jane's visits away from home were to prove invaluable for her writing in another way. As she got older she frequently stayed, often on her own and for fairly long periods of time, in a variety of homes. These included a number of different rectories,[10] enabling her to widen her experience of parish life and different members of the clergy, whom she could watch both in their parish roles and in social settings. She often spent periods of time with her brother Edward and his growing family in their various homes, as he moved up the social scale, finally becoming the aristocratic squire of Godmersham and Chawton in 1797. She made a few visits to Bath, sometimes staying with her aunt and uncle in the Walcot area of the city, other times staying in rented lodgings with other family members. These first experiences of Bath were to play a key role in the work that we know today as *Northanger Abbey*.

Some critics describe her world view as small. Jane was determined to write only of that which she knew, her "three or four families in a country village", but her own experience of staying in different homes of the gentry and within the aristocratic world of her day enabled her to write with assurance of life in different social settings in her novels, such as Mr Collins' "humble" Hunsford Parsonage, the Bennet family home in Longbourn, the grander house at Netherfield, and the even grander Pemberley, all within *Pride and Prejudice*.

Jane's Romantic Experiences

I will be arguing in the course of this book that Jane Austen's novels are about so much more than love and marriage, but on the surface that is what they primarily seem to cover. So it is appropriate to explore Jane's early experiences of romance, to see how they might have shaped her as a writer of novels about young women falling in love. Playful references to Tom Lefroy, written in a letter to Cassandra in January 1796 when she was twenty, are the only words we have from Jane herself about any affair of her heart. Tom was the Irish nephew of her friend and neighbour Anne Lefroy of Ashe:

> *You scold me so much in the nice long letter which I have this moment received from you, that I am almost afraid to tell you how my Irish friend and I behaved. Imagine to yourself everything most profligate and shocking in the way of dancing and sitting down together. **I can** expose myself however, only **once more**, because he leaves the country soon after next Friday, on which day we **are** to have a dance at Ashe after all. He is a very gentlemanlike, good-looking, pleasant young man, I assure you. But as to our having ever met, except at the three last balls, I cannot say much; for he is so excessively laughed at about me at Ashe, that he is ashamed of coming to Steventon, and ran away when we called on Mrs. Lefroy a few days ago.[11]*

What looks to be most likely is that Tom, who had just completed a degree in Ireland and was about to study for the bar, was discouraged by his family from forming a closer relationship with Jane, as she had nothing to offer financially and he needed to marry for money. So he was whisked away from Hampshire back to Ireland and the two of them never met again. He married a Wexford heiress a few years later. As an old man he confessed that Jane Austen was his first love. We do not know how sorely she grieved her loss or whether she was as sanguine as Elizabeth Bennet, to whom, on perceiving Mr Wickham moving from her to the heiress Miss King, Jane gives the words "handsome young men must have something to live on, as well as the plain".

Soon after Jane's abortive relationship with Tom Lefroy, Cassandra's engagement ended in tragedy. Her fiancé, Revd Tom Fowle, died of fever in the West Indies where he had gone to be a private chaplain to Lord Craven, who was an army colonel. It seems that Cassandra then turned her face against any possibility of loving and marrying anyone else and accepted her unmarried lot with resolution.[12]

In all her novels, Jane Austen's heroines marry for love, but they also know they need to be able to respect and be respected by their husband. With her great skills of observation and discernment, she would doubtless have formed her views on the different states of marriage from her own family's experiences and from those of the many families and friends with whom she stayed, especially so as she was often with them in their homes for long periods of time.

Events in Jane's Family

Jane did not grow up untouched or unaffected by the world outside her neighbourhood. There were events of great drama within her own family, which took place in India, France, and England. Through relations of both her mother and her father, Jane had a link with Warren Hastings, who became Governor General of India in 1773, before being impeached in 1787 and finally acquitted after a long trial in 1795. He had known the Leighs of Adlestrop, cousins to Mrs Cassandra Austen, from his childhood. Eleven years before Jane was born, Hastings' only child, the seven-year-old motherless George, who had been sent to England in the care of the Leigh family, came to live with the Austens, but died of diphtheria shortly afterwards. Meanwhile, in 1753 Jane's father's sister, Philadelphia, who had been sent to India to find a husband, had married Tysoe Saul Hancock, who was a surgeon with the East India Company and a friend and business associate of Warren Hastings. Philadelphia's flamboyant daughter, Eliza, her only child, was born in 1861, nine years after the marriage, and was believed by many to be Hastings' illegitimate child. Eliza was Hastings' god-daughter, and he set up a trust fund for her, which was eventually administered by George Austen. Eliza named her only son Hastings after him. Though the major public events of Warren Hastings' life took place in the years before we have any letters written by Jane, the Austen family must have followed his career with great interest, for Jane refers to him several times in later letters.[13]

Eliza moved to England from India as a child and later married a Frenchman, Jean de Feuillide, whom she always claimed was a count. He was arrested and guillotined during the Terror following the French Revolution in 1794, when Jane was nineteen. Eliza was a frequent visitor to Steventon throughout Jane's girlhood, and she contemplated marrying the family's eldest son, James, in 1796. She was fourteen years older than Jane, and no doubt a source of great fascination to her precocious young cousin, bringing a taste of danger, drama, and the exotic with her on her visits to Steventon.

There was drama too when Jane's mother's brother's wife, Jane Leigh-Perrot, was arrested in 1799 in a shop near the Pump Room in Bath, and charged with shoplifting a piece of lace. She was held in Somerset County Gaol in Ilchester while awaiting trial, though because of her position in society she did not have to wear prison uniform and she lodged with the prison keeper's family. Jane Austen's mother wrote offering for Jane, then aged twenty-four, to come to Ilchester to keep her aunt company, but the offer was declined, as Mrs Leigh-Perrot did not think it would be a suitable experience for her niece. After seven months she went to court at Taunton. The family knew she could face the death penalty if found guilty, though it was much more likely, given her social status, that she would have been transported to Australia. It was decided at the trial, however, that the charge had been trumped up by the shopkeeper, in an attempt to blackmail Mr Leigh-Perrot.

The Historical Context of the Times

Jane was living at Steventon during the time of the French Revolution, which took place between 1789 and 1799. France went from a monarchy headed by King Louis XVI to a republic supposedly ruled by the people, and then to the dictatorship of Napoleon Bonaparte. This period was one of the bloodiest in European history, and the social structure of France was overthrown. Louis XVI was guillotined in 1793, and then the Reign of Terror saw the deaths of tens of thousands of people, particularly from the land-owning and aristocratic classes. As we have seen, Jane Austen's cousin's husband was among them. France also declared war on the United Kingdom, and the threat of invasion remained until France, under Napoleon, was finally decisively defeated at the Battle of Waterloo in 1815. So war, or the threat of war, hung over most of Jane's life. Some critics denigrate her because she does not overtly reflect the fear or the reality of war in her novels, all of which had contemporary settings. A regiment is quartered for the winter at Meryton in *Pride and Prejudice*, but no military training is described, and almost the only threat to the local residents is from the ill-disciplined behaviour of some of the officers. She would have been aware of what was going on, however: the local press in Steventon was full of reports of murder, rape, and burglary committed by soldiers, and there were two military encampments in the area, one in Andover and one in Basingstoke, plus many French prisoners of war. So it seems that Jane Austen deliberately chose to avoid the subject of war in her books.

The French Revolution and war with France had wider social consequences in Britain. As they heard the news of the annihilation of the French upper classes and the social chaos all over France, many of the British aristocracy feared that political unrest on this side of the Channel threatened their safe way of life.[14] There were also more demands for social change among the lower classes.[15] The Church of England, with its presence and influence in every community, was seen by the more thoughtful in society to have a key role in discouraging revolt.[16] Clergy and other leaders were not only expected to uphold and encourage the members of the gentry in their influence for good in society, but they were to teach the lower orders to accept the order of things.

Writing Novels

There was no shortage of new novels being published in Jane's lifetime, and by the time she was in her early twenties and beginning to write her first full-length book, novel reading was an established habit for large sections of the population.[17] Many of the authors of these novels were women who were able to publish freely under their own name. In this respect the Georgian period was a much more liberal time for women than the Victorian era that followed, when many women writers, including Anne, Charlotte, and Emily Brontë and Mary Anne Evans, felt the necessity to assume men's names – Acton, Currer, and Ellis Bell and George Eliot, respectively. It was quite natural, therefore, at that time, for Jane Austen to consider that she too might write novels and become a published author, and, although she also chose to be anonymous, her gender was not disguised.

As we have seen, there was at the time a particular craze, among women writers in particular, to make their stories more exciting by setting them not in the real world but in the fantasy worlds of the Gothic and Romantic Sentimental genres. Not surprisingly, therefore, novels came to be regarded by some people as frivolous, and even dangerous to the young women reading them. Though she critiqued and parodied both the Gothic novel and the Romantic Sentimental novel in her *Juvenilia* and her early novels *Northanger Abbey* and *Sense and Sensibility*, Jane Austen remained, in her own words, an "unashamed novel reader", and she ensured that many of her principal heroines and heroes were as well.

So in *Northanger Abbey* the novel's anti-hero, John Thorpe, declares: "Oh, Lord! not I; I never read novels; I have something else to do," but the hero, clergyman Henry Tilney, is heard to observe: "The person, be it gentleman or lady, who has not pleasure in a good novel, must be intolerably stupid." "Intolerably stupid" is indeed how Jane Austen depicts Mr Collins, the clergyman in *Pride and Prejudice*. On his first day at Longbourn, Mr Bennet initially responds with the keenest enjoyment to his guest's absurdities, but

[b]y tea-time, however, the dose had been enough, and Mr. Bennet was glad to take his guest into the drawing-room again, and, when tea was over, glad to invite him to read aloud to the ladies.

> *Mr. Collins readily assented, and a book was produced; but on*
> *beholding it, (for everything announced it to be from a circulating*
> *library) he started back, and begging pardon, protested that he*
> *never read novels. Kitty stared at him, and Lydia exclaimed.*
> *Other books were produced, and after some deliberation he chose*
> *Fordyce's Sermons.*

A sermon from Revd James Fordyce was an appropriate choice
for the critical Mr Collins. Jane Austen may well have had in
mind a sermon from Fordyce's *Sermons to Young Women*, possibly
the very one in which Fordyce declared: "[T]here seem to be
very few, in the style of a Novel, that you can read with safety,
and yet fewer that you can read with advantage."[18] Not all
clergymen agreed with such a sentiment, however. Jane's father,
Revd George Austen, certainly did not.

Contrary to the views of Bishop Fordyce and the opinions
she put into the mouth of Mr Collins, Jane Austen was to write
novels that she believed young women could read with safety,
and that readers, male and female, young and old, could read
with advantage. She did indeed believe that reading could be
"useful". For in *Northanger Abbey* Jane Austen defends the novel
in the strongest terms, and reveals her understanding of the
purpose of a novel. After saying that Catherine and Isabella
read novels together, she continues:

> *Yes, novels; for I will not adopt that ungenerous and impolitic*
> *custom, so common with novel writers, of degrading, by their*
> *contemptuous censure, the very performances to the number of*
> *which they are themselves adding: joining with their greatest*
> *enemies in bestowing the harshest epithets on such works, and*
> *scarcely ever permitting them to be read by their own heroine,*
> *who, if she accidentally take up a novel, is sure to turn over its*
> *insipid pages with disgust. Alas! if the heroine of one novel be not*

patronized by the heroine of another, from whom can she expect
protection and regard? I cannot approve of it. Let us leave it to
the Reviewers to abuse such effusions of fancy at their leisure, and
over every new novel to talk in thread-bare strains of the trash
with which the press now groans. Let us not desert one another;
we are an injured body. Although our productions have afforded
more extensive and unaffected pleasure than those of any other
literary corporation in the world, no species of composition has
been so much decried. From pride, ignorance, or fashion, our foes
are almost as many as our readers,...

Jane Austen set out to write novels in which (in her own words) she brought the "greatest powers of her mind" to bear on displaying a "thorough knowledge of human nature". Though her novels were written with the "liveliest effusions of wit and humour" and indeed "are conveyed to the world in the best chosen language", she wanted them to be useful to her readers – to enable them to reflect, as did her principal heroines and heroes, on the nature of their moral responsibilities.

The increasing length and the growing creative maturity of her fiction writings in her *Juvenilia* led Jane Austen to have the confidence to begin to write longer pieces of work. The first drafts of three of her six novels were written during the Steventon years: *Elinor and Marianne* was written in 1795 when she was nineteen, and then rewritten under the title *Sense and Sensibility* in 1797. *First Impressions*, the first draft of *Pride and Prejudice*, was written between October 1796 and August 1797 when Jane was twenty-one; and *Susan,* which in time became *Northanger Abbey*, was begun in 1798, with its first draft finished in 1799.

Although we are aware from Jane's letters, and from the later recollections of her family, of the dates when these first drafts were written, only the final manuscripts of *Sense and Sensibility*,

Pride and Prejudice, and *Northanger Abbey* (each of which dates from some years after Jane had left Steventon) exist today, so we can only speculate about how much she changed them in later years. However, as her three later novels, *Mansfield Park*, *Emma*, and *Persuasion*, which were both begun and finished when she was in her thirties and early forties, reflect deeper themes and have a more complex social context, we can take the early three novels as emerging from her Steventon life.

CHAPTER THREE

THE EARLY NOVELS:
SENSE AND SENSIBILITY,
PRIDE AND PREJUDICE,
AND *NORTHANGER ABBEY*

Sense and Sensibility

Sense and Sensibility tells the story of two sisters, Elinor and Marianne Dashwood. When the novel opens, they, with their mother and much younger sister Margaret, have just lost their father, and their home, Norland Park, has been inherited by their older stepbrother, John, and his wife, Fanny. The Dashwood family have to leave and move to Barton Cottage in Devon, on the estate of a distant relative, Sir John Middleton. Both girls fall in love – Elinor with Fanny Dashwood's brother, Edward Ferrars, and Marianne with the dashing country gentleman John Willoughby – and then both face the loss of their love. The two sisters have very different characters, however, and the focus of the story is on the very different ways in which they react to love and to loss.

Jane Austen began this work in 1795, naming it *Elinor and Marianne* and writing it in epistolary form. The manuscript is now lost but we can conjecture that the very different content and styles of the letters, written by her two very different heroines, would have enabled her to distinguish clearly their very different approaches to life. She must, however, have found this method too constricting, as she never again attempted an epistolary novel and she rewrote her manuscript a couple of years later in a narrated story format under the new title *Sense and Sensibility*. Instead of naming the story after her two main characters, she decided to name it after two virtues, indicating that virtue is an important theme in the novel.

We saw in the last chapter that Jane particularly enjoyed reading the novels of Samuel Richardson, one of which was called *Pamela: or, Virtue Rewarded*, and that her declared favourite novel was Richardson's *Sir Charles Grandison*, which stressed the importance of the virtues.[1] The development of virtue reflects the importance of morality, which, as we have seen, was an intrinsic part of Jane's Anglican upbringing. It is important to understand the meanings of the virtues "sense" and "sensibility" in the context of the eighteenth-century world. "Sense" expressed a respect for order, logic, and rational control. When rightly used, sense brought balance and self-control. When used to excess, however, with no balancing sensibility, then sense could lead to callousness and rigidity. "Sensibility" meant having emotional awareness, with a sensitivity to pleasure and pain, beauty and ugliness. It is at the extreme end of such a sensibility that Jane Austen is most mocking of those who pride themselves on being more sensitive than their fellow beings, but are in fact behaving with great self-centredness, concerned only with their own feelings. In the novel she explores how sense and sensibility must be kept in balance in a virtuous life.

Sense and sensibility are examined in the interplay of the characters in the novel, and especially within the close family circle of the Dashwoods. In the opening chapter, shortly after the death of Mr Dashwood, we read:

Elinor saw, with concern, the excess of her sister's sensibility; but by Mrs Dashwood it was valued and cherished. They encouraged each other now in the violence of their affliction. The agony of grief which overpowered them at first, was voluntarily renewed, was sought for, was created again and again. They gave themselves wholly up to their sorrow, seeking increase of wretchedness in every reflection that could afford it, and resolved against ever admitting consolation in future. Elinor, too, was deeply afflicted; but still she could struggle, she could exert herself. She could consult with her brother, could receive her sister-in-law on arrival, and treat her with proper attention; and could strive to rouse her mother to similar exertion, and encourage her to similar forbearance.

Marianne and her mother, at the beginning of the novel, are all sensibility – and although Mrs Dashwood can be galvanized by Elinor on occasion to show some sense, Marianne can never be. When Marianne meets the dashingly handsome and apparently rich John Willoughby, in the romantic hillside setting where he rescues her after a fall, and finds that he is a fellow lover of poetry and novels, she falls in love with a passion so intense that she flouts the current social conventions of her day: she spends time with him alone, allows him to take a lock of her hair, and is eager to receive his lavish and improper gift of a horse. When Willoughby then abandons and forsakes her, Marianne gives herself up to a grief so inconsolable that she is unable to be civil to those around her:

She was awake the whole night, and she wept the greatest part of it. She got up with an headache, was unable to talk, and unwilling to take any nourishment; giving pain every moment to her mother and sisters, and forbidding all attempt at consolation from either.

After a long stay in London, where Marianne can still barely bring herself to speak to those who show her much kindness, events enable her to realize something of the selfishness of her excessive sensibility. She has accused Elinor of coldness and lack of empathy, but when she is finally told about Edward's engagement to Lucy Steele she realizes Elinor's inner strength – for Elinor has borne her loss in private and has continued to care for Marianne and others, despite her anguish. Marianne so admires this resolve that she determines to be more like her sister. On the journey home, however, another bout of self-pity overwhelms her and drives her out into the rain, and she nearly dies from pneumonia as a result. This near-death experience finally shocks her into self-reflection and change. In time, she accepts Colonel Brandon's proposal of marriage, despite having dismissed him earlier as too old.

Jane Austen's heroine and heroes in this novel, Elinor, Edward, and Colonel Brandon, combine sense and sensibility – we see them develop and grow. Elinor appears outwardly to be all sense because she has mastered self-control, but while Marianne is initially unable to see Elinor's loss we, the readers, can recognize it and perceive her sensibility in the inner anguish such loss causes her. Yet she continues to be the competent leader of the household. It is through Elinor's influence and example that Marianne is able to learn from her mistakes and change. Edward, in accordance with the expectations of a man of honour of his day, keeps his loveless engagement to the social-climbing Lucy Steele. His development is in finding the courage to stand up to his mother and make his own way in life without her financial support. Jane Austen leads her readers to conclude that having a good character involves developing a healthy combination of both sense and sensibility. Those with excessive sensibility, however, are treated with compassion if they can learn from the past and gain some sense. Thus

Marianne is rewarded for the self-reflection that has led to her changing and becoming more self-controlled, by her marriage to the generous Colonel Brandon. Willoughby, whom we learn at the end of the novel really did love Marianne, appears to confess his faults, is forgiven by Elinor, and is allowed to live a not totally unhappy life in his loveless marriage to Miss Grey.

It is those with excessive sense, who gain no balancing sensibility through the course of the narrative, who receive the most criticism from their author: the scheming Lucy Steele and the avaricious John and Fanny Dashwood are offered no redemption. At the beginning of the novel, Jane Austen lets Fanny Dashwood persuade her husband out of giving anything from their father's estate to his half-sisters:

> *Do but consider, my dear Mr Dashwood, how excessively comfortable your mother-in-law and her daughters may live on the interest of seven thousand pounds, besides the thousand pounds belonging to each of the girls, which brings them in fifty pounds a-year a-piece, and, of course, they will pay their mother for their board out of it. Altogether, they will have five hundred a-year amongst them, and what on earth can four women want for more than that? – They will live so cheap! Their housekeeping will be nothing at all. They will have no carriage, no horses, and hardly any servants; they will keep no company, and can have no expenses of any kind! Only conceive how comfortable they will be! I am sure I cannot imagine how they will spend half of it; and as to your giving them more, it is quite absurd to think of it. They will be much more able to give **you** something.*

In the final chapter John Dashwood expresses envy of Marianne and suggests to his wife that they should regularly receive the Brandons in their home – not because he admires Colonel Brandon but because he recognizes that Brandon has a house and park that are grander than his own. However, he does not mention his other half-sister Elinor, now happily married to his wife's brother, Revd Edward Ferrars, who is set to inherit only a small part of the Ferrars family fortune. John and Fanny Dashwood have not changed through the course of the novel; they remain all sense and no sensibility, and Jane Austen leaves them as they were at the start of the story – materialistic and greedy.

We see in *Sense and Sensibility* important themes that link strongly with our understanding of spirituality. Primarily in this novel Jane Austen stresses the importance of achieving the right balance – finding a harmony in life between sense and sensibility. This sense of right balance is also, of course, an inherent part of the nature of the Anglicanism in which she grew up, as practised by her father. Other important values are treated favourably in the novel, especially Elinor's moral influence and Edward's duty in keeping to his engagement until his fiancée breaks it, which would be deemed both honourable and commendable at that time. The materialism shared by Lucy, John, and Fanny is contrasted with the contentment of Elinor and Marianne, who are lifted to a higher realm of love and possibility.

The place of an inner path is explored in depth in the novel. Marianne has always had an inner life, and has engaged deeply with nature, poetry, and music, but these have taken her too far into herself, enabling her to get caught up more and more in her own feelings and passions – and this self-indulgence can be dangerous, Jane Austen warns us. By the end of the novel Marianne has learned to engage in a more balanced self-reflection that takes her out of her self-centredness, enables her to see what is good in other people, compels her to consider them, and empowers her to change. Now she can recognize and value the solid love of Colonel Brandon.

Elinor and Marianne's experiences of loss followed by inner

growth leading to new life, mirror the biblical story at the heart of the Christian faith – death and resurrection. The story's structure therefore reflects a strong biblical theme.

Pride and Prejudice

The first draft of *Pride and Prejudice*, widely held to be Jane Austen's most famous and popular novel, was written when she was just twenty-one and, as we have seen, she originally titled the manuscript *First Impressions*. In its final form, *Pride and Prejudice* tells the story of the "first impressions" formed by Elizabeth Bennet and Mr Darcy when they first meet, and of how, in time, they overcome these first impressions. Darcy's initial reaction to Elizabeth in particular, but also to the company in and around Meryton, is governed by pride. His behaviour causes her to dismiss him, and thus to be prejudiced against him when they meet again. Eventually they find deep and mutual love and respect for each other.

Their first encounter takes place at a country ball at an inn in Meryton, an occasion far beneath Darcy's customary social setting. He is the owner of the magnificent estate of Pemberley in Derbyshire and has an income of ten thousand pounds a year. When encouraged to dance with Elizabeth by his friend Mr Bingley, Darcy replies: "She is tolerable; but not handsome enough to tempt *me*; and I am in no humour at present to give consequence to young ladies who are slighted by other men." Elizabeth feels belittled, and the next day she declares to her mother: "I may safely promise you *never* to dance with him," and then adds: "I could easily forgive *his* pride, if he had not mortified *mine*."

Very soon afterwards Elizabeth meets and feels very drawn to Mr Wickham, who, in contrast to Darcy, is all openness and friendliness. Elizabeth, who prides herself on being a good judge of character, readily believes all that he tells her of Darcy's pride and cruel behaviour towards him in the past. Her prejudice grows in consequence. However, Darcy finds himself to be enormously attracted by Elizabeth, although his pride means he still revolts against the behaviour of most of her close family, and their status overall. In his first proposal, he is blunt about his sense of her social inferiority: "Could you expect me to rejoice in the inferiority of your connections? To congratulate myself on the hope of relations, whose condition in life is so decidedly beneath my own?" he asks, after she has roundly rejected him.

Elizabeth goes on to accuse him of separating her sister Jane from Mr Bingley because of the Bennet family's inferior social connections, and of damaging Wickham's career prospects. In his long letter in reply, Darcy first explains how, although her mother's family connections are an obstacle, they are nothing compared with "the total want of propriety" so often shown by Mrs Bennet, the three younger sisters (Mary, Kitty, and Lydia), and occasionally by her father. And he reveals the duplicitous and perfidious behaviour of George Wickham, both to him and to his sister, Georgiana, the details of which he has previously kept entirely within his immediate family. There is a very touching ending to Darcy's letter to Elizabeth. Before he signs his name, he writes: "I will only add, God bless you." Whatever Elizabeth's response to his letter and to him might be, by invoking God's blessing upon her he shows that he does not wish to see her hurt. He wishes her well, seeking the best for her life, despite the anguish that she has caused him.

There follows a long period of self-reflection for Elizabeth as she acknowledges the humiliating justification of Darcy's comments about her family's behaviour, and begins to change her understanding of and her attitude towards him:

She grew absolutely ashamed of herself. Of neither Darcy nor Wickham could she think without feeling that she had been blind, partial, prejudiced, absurd. "How despicably have I acted!" she cried. "I, who have prided myself on my discernment! I, who have valued myself on my abilities! who have often disdained the generous candour of my sister, and gratified my vanity in useless or blameable distrust. How humiliating is this discovery! Yet, how just a humiliation! Had I been in love, I could not have been more wretchedly blind."

By the end of the novel we see that Darcy, too, has reflected long and hard on his attitudes, and that he has allowed Elizabeth to change him:

"Your reproof, so well applied, I shall never forget: 'Had you behaved in a more gentlemanlike manner.' Those were your words. You know not, you can scarcely conceive, how they have tortured me; though it was some time, I confess, before I was reasonable enough to allow their justice."

The characters of Lydia and Wickham, by contrast, remain unchanged throughout the novel. Lydia is loud, impetuous, greedy, and completely self-centred from beginning to end. When she receives an invitation to accompany the regiment to Brighton, one not extended to Kitty, we hear that

[w]holly inattentive to her sister's feelings, Lydia flew about the house in restless ecstasy, calling for everyone's congratulations, and laughing and talking with more violence than ever...

Jane Austen tells us that Lydia "seldom listened to anybody for more than half a minute..." and she has no ability to reflect. When she and Wickham are invited to visit Longbourn after their hastily arranged wedding, she is oblivious to all the anguish and scandal her affair has caused. In the hearing of all of her family, she asks:

> *"Oh! mamma, do the people hereabouts know I am married today! I was afraid they might not; and we overtook William Goulding in his curricle, so I was determined he should know it, and so I let down the side glass next to him, and took off my glove and let my hand just rest upon the window frame, so that he might see the ring; and then I bowed and smiled like anything."*

Wickham's affair with Lydia shows he has not reformed since Darcy discovered his earlier plot to elope with Georgiana. His behaviour at Longbourn, like Lydia's, reveals no shame for what he has done. As Mr Bennet satirically comments, "He simpers, and smirks, and makes love to us all. I am prodigiously proud of him. I defy even Sir William Lucas himself to produce a more valuable son-in-law."

There is, however, more hope for Kitty Bennet. Kitty does not have the strength of character of Jane and Elizabeth, who have each managed to develop good character and morals despite their unpromising home life. Kitty has also been too influenced by Lydia. After her sisters' marriages, however,

> *Kitty, to her very material advantage, spent the chief of her time with her two elder sisters. In society so superior to what she had generally known, her improvement was great. She was not of so ungovernable a temper as Lydia; and, removed from the influence of Lydia's example, she became, by proper attention and management, less irritable, less ignorant and less insipid.*

Mary Bennet also is left at the end of the novel with hope of improvement. Mary is not self-aware, so when she plays and sings at the Netherfield Ball she is unaware of the low standard of her playing and the embarrassment that she causes her family. She is a great reader of sermons and other moral and pious writings. However, she is unable to apply her reading to everyday life. In the course of a family discussion about social etiquette, Mr Bennet asks:

> *"What say you, Mary? For you are a young lady of deep*
> *reflection I know, and read great books, and make extracts."*
> *Mary wished to say something very sensible, but knew not how.*

Mary's reading does not lead to wise judgments, so it does not enable her to offer help or hope to others. So, after Lydia's elopement, she can only quote moral platitudes, not practical advice:

> *"Unhappy as the event must be for Lydia, we may draw from it*
> *this useful lesson: that loss of virtue in a female is irretrievable;*
> *that one false step involves her in endless ruin; that her reputation*
> *is no less brittle than it is beautiful; and that she cannot be too*
> *much guarded in her behaviour towards the undeserving of the*
> *other sex."*

At the end of the novel Mary is the only sister left at Longbourn. Mrs Bennet's need for company, both at home and on social visits, obliges her to mix more with the world, "and as she was no longer mortified by comparisons between her sisters' beauty and her own, it was suspected by her father that she submitted to the change without much reluctance". Jane Austen makes it clear that this is not a substantive change of character, for Mary could still "moralize over every morning visit". However, with both Mary and Kitty, Jane Austen shows that, with a change of environment, their characters can be improved.

A parallel theme of the book explores how people are perceived by others – the contrast between a person's outer appearance and their inner character. When Elizabeth finally understands the good character of Darcy, as compared to the bad character of Wickham, she concludes: "One has got all the goodness, and the other all the appearance of it."

A turning point in Elizabeth's understanding of the character of Mr Darcy is her visit to Pemberley. Later, she is jokingly to tell Jane that she first began to love Darcy when she saw his beautiful grounds at Pemberley – but the novel makes it clear that, while on a tour of the house with the housekeeper, it was what Mrs Reynolds said of Mr Darcy's character that principally entranced her, not the outer appearance of the good taste and wealth of the house and grounds:

"His father was an excellent man," said Mrs Gardiner. "Yes, Ma'am, that he was indeed; and his son will be just like him – just as affable to the poor."

Later in the tour of the house, as they come to the picture gallery and Elizabeth finds that only the portrait of Mr Darcy can arrest her attention, she reflects on what she has heard from the housekeeper:

The commendation bestowed on him by Mrs Reynolds was of no trifling nature. What praise is more valuable than the praise of an intelligent servant? As a brother, a landlord, a master, she considered how many people's happiness were in his guardianship! ... Every idea that had been brought forward by the housekeeper was favourable to his character, and as she stood before the canvas, on which he was represented, and fixed his eyes upon herself, she thought of his regard with a deeper sentiment of gratitude than it had ever raised before; she remembered its warmth, and softened its impropriety of expression.

Elizabeth now knows that Darcy is at heart a good man, but that he has to learn to overcome the pride that has come from his privileged position in society. He needs to begin to display a more gracious manner to the world outside the social circle of Pemberley, to practise the virtue of civility as well as honesty, and to show generosity as well as justice. But Darcy has come to recognize this himself, as he confesses to Elizabeth at the end of the novel:

> *"I have been a selfish being all my life, in practice, though not in principle. As a child I was taught what was **right**, but I was not taught to correct my temper. I was given good principles, but left to follow them in pride and conceit... my parents... allowed, encouraged, almost taught me to be selfish and overbearing, to care for none beyond my own family circle, to think meanly of all the rest of the world, to **wish** at least to think meanly of their sense and worth compared to my own. Such I was, from eight to eight and twenty; and such I might still have been but for you, dearest, loveliest Elizabeth! What do I not owe you! ... By you, I was properly humbled."*

Elizabeth's maternal uncle and aunt Mr and Mrs Gardiner play a key role in demonstrating the change in Darcy. Elizabeth is very close to the Gardiners – they are people of great respectability and good sense, and they provide her with much better parental models than do her own parents. Before we meet them, though, the Gardiners have already been spoken of most disparagingly by Miss Bingley, for they live on the unfashionable Cheapside in London, where Mr Gardiner not only engages in trade but lives within view of his own warehouses. After Elizabeth and the Gardiners have heard the profuse praise of Mrs Reynolds at Pemberley, they meet Mr Darcy, who has come home earlier than he was expected. He asks Elizabeth if she will introduce him to "her friends":

"What will be his surprise," thought she, "when he knows who they are! He takes them now for people of fashion." The introduction, however, was immediately made; and as she named their relationship to herself, she stole a sly look at him, to see how he bore it; and was not without the expectation of his decamping as fast as he could from such disgraceful companions. That he was **surprised** *by the connexion was evident; he sustained it, however, with fortitude, and, so far from going away, turned back with them, and entered into conversation with Mr Gardiner.*

Within a day the Gardiners have been invited to an evening at Pemberley, much to the disgust of Miss Bingley, who is also present but whose protestations are ignored. Later, Darcy enters into an alliance with them as he and Mr Gardiner seek out the runaways, Lydia and Wickham, in London and arrange their marriage. It is touching and indicative of the change within Darcy that the very last sentences of the novel are given to the Gardiners and concern the newly married Mr and Mrs Darcy's shared esteem and love for them:

With the Gardiners, they were always on the most intimate terms. Darcy, as well as Elizabeth, really loved them; and they were both ever sensible of the warmest gratitude towards the persons who, by bringing her into Derbyshire, had been the means of uniting them.

Jane Austen famously begins her novel with the sardonic words:

It is a truth universally acknowledged, that a single man in possession of a good fortune must be in want of a wife.

It follows on from this that a recurrent theme of the book is money: the need for money and the attitudes of her characters to those with and without money. So, in the Bennet household, where the girls will have little fortune and the house and property and the bulk of the money are entailed and will be left to Mr Collins, it is not surprising that the constantly anxious Mrs Bennet is so desperate to see her daughters married to men of good fortune. Elizabeth resolves that she will not marry only for money. She will only marry someone whom she can love and respect. Her more pragmatic friend Charlotte Lucas chooses differently, engineering her own marriage to Mr Collins, whom Elizabeth has just rejected, to ensure that she will have a secure, if loveless, home for her future.

Through the course of the novel we see whether or not people are contented, being grateful for what they have and able to share it generously. The Gardiners, as we have seen, are not as rich as some others in the novel, for Mr Gardiner has to work for his living, but they live with great contentment. Mr Wickham, however, is never satisfied or able to make good with what he has, and is always seeking more. This does not change on his marriage and, even after a generous settlement from Mr Darcy and despite employment having been found for him with a northern army regiment, he and Lydia cannot live within their means and they still regularly apply to Elizabeth for more money. The Bingley family have made their money recently through trade (which Miss Bingley conveniently forgets in her criticisms of the Gardiners) – but there is a great contrast between the generous, warm-hearted Bingley and his mean-spirited sister Caroline. Another rich character, Lady Catherine de Bourgh, is disdainful of all below her in wealth and rank, and has a high opinion of herself. We hear this when, jealous of those gathering around the piano to hear Elizabeth play, she declares: "There are few people in England, I suppose, who have more true enjoyment of music than myself, or a better natural taste. If I had ever learnt, I should have been a great proficient." She also shows a complete lack of concern for other people's feelings, as we hear in her invitation to Elizabeth to practise on the pianoforte in Mrs Jenkinson's room, where, states Lady Catherine, "She would be in nobody's way… in that part of the house."

Lady Catherine and her protégé, the fawning and pompous Mr Collins, when seen as comic characters, are widely enjoyed by readers of *Pride and Prejudice*. While Jane Austen suggests no criticism of the faith of the Christianity they represent, implicit in the text are criticisms of the church, as an institution, that can allow such people to be in positions of power and influence as clergy and as patrons. Mr Collins, we learn, "was not a sensible man, and the deficiency of nature had been but little assisted by education or society; the greatest part of his life having been spent under the guidance of an illiterate and miserly father; and though he belonged to one of the universities, he had merely kept the necessary terms, without forming at it any useful acquaintance". He is presented as lacking the character and integrity needed to be a moral influence for good in his parish. Moreover, he appears to have no spiritual understanding of his role and calling: "the respect which he felt for her (Lady Catherine's) high rank, and his veneration for her as his patroness, mingling with a very good opinion of himself, of his authority as a clergyman, and his rights as a rector, made him altogether a mixture of pride and obsequiousness, self-importance and humility."

Nor does his faith show up well. His first harsh letter to Mr Bennet after Lydia's elopement reveals his selfish relief at having escaped from an engagement to Elizabeth the previous year, and he offers no pastoral or spiritual support to the family:

> *"The death of your daughter would have been a blessing in comparison of this… I am inclined to think that her own*

*disposition must be naturally bad, or she could not be guilty
of such an enormity, at so early an age... this false step in one
daughter will be injurious to the fortunes of all the others; for
who, as Lady Catherine herself condescendingly says, will connect
themselves with such a family? And this consideration leads me
moreover to reflect, with augmented satisfaction, on a certain event
of last November; for had it been otherwise, I must have been
involved in all your sorrow and disgrace. Let me advise you then,
my dear Sir, to console yourself as much as possible, to throw off
your unworthy child from your affection for ever, and leave her to
reap the fruits of her own heinous offence."*

Later he writes: "You ought certainly to forgive them, as a
Christian, but never to admit them in your sight, or allow their
names to be mentioned in your hearing." In response, Mr
Bennet comments: "*That* is his notion of Christian forgiveness!"
So through the novel there is implicit criticism of the church as
an institution that permits men like Mr Collins to find a career.
Elizabeth Bennet also recognizes with concern that Wickham
had at one point in his life declared his intention of being
ordained, and she asks him: "How should you have liked making
sermons?" Wickham's response is about the duty and exertion of
writing sermons, and about the quiet and retirement of the life
of the clergy, but the implication of Elizabeth's question is that
sermons give a moral lead to others, something she recognizes
Wickham is incapable of doing.

In terms of our three criteria of spirituality, *Pride and Prejudice*
scores highly as a spiritual book. Jane Austen has a lot to say
about values as she stresses the importance of inner character as
opposed to outward appearance. The virtues that are particularly
commended throughout the book are civility, responsibility,
generosity, and goodness. An important part of responsibility
is moral influence. Those in a position to influence others –

such as Darcy as a landowner, Mr Collins as a clergyman, Lady Catherine as a patron, and Mr and Mrs Bennet as parents – should recognize their responsibility to others and be an example by their words and actions, though not all of them manage to do so.

The subject of materialism is explored through self-contentment – those who are content with what they have can find an inner peace, which eludes those who are continually seeking more. Self-reflection, as we have seen, is a central part of the novel – when practised by both Darcy and Elizabeth, it leads to a recognition of their faults (specifically those of pride and prejudice), and they change to become better people. Again, this change is both outward and community-facing – this is apparent in the last chapter. They change, their marriage is possible, and it brings change for the better to members of their families and, it is implied, to all within the Pemberley estate.

In *Pride and Prejudice* we can again trace the biblical themes of death and resurrection, of loss and redemption. At Hunsford Darcy has to begin to come to terms with loss after Elizabeth's abrupt refusal of his marriage proposal. Elizabeth's realizations of loss come firstly when she confronts her failings as she reads Darcy's letter, and secondly when she recognizes her love for Darcy after the visit to Pemberley – scarcely has she acknowledged her feelings to herself before she learns of Lydia's elopement and the disgrace this has brought upon her family. At this point, realization strikes: "[N]ever had she so honestly felt that she could have loved him, as now, when all love must be in vain." However, it is through their loss that the self-reflection comes which leads, for Elizabeth and Darcy, to the transformation of their characters, and, finally, to the reward of new life through shared mutual love. But, for characters such as Wickham and Lydia, Mr Collins and Lady Catherine, who are all unable or unwilling to admit they need to change, there can be no transformation and therefore no expectation of future love or happiness.

Northanger Abbey

Throughout *Northanger Abbey* we see Jane Austen mocking the genres of the Romantic Sentimental and Gothic novel. This is apparent from the first sentence: "No one who had ever seen Catherine Morland in her infancy, would have supposed her born to be a heroine. Her situation in life, the character of her father and mother; her own person and disposition, were all equally against her." Jane Austen makes clear in this opening sentence that, to her, Catherine is a heroine, even if she is not a heroine according to the requirements of the Gothic or Romantic Sentimental novel. Such novels required a prescriptive background that was necessary for a character's heroism, which included a childhood fraught with disasters and obstacles that had already been overcome. In what sense, then, Jane Austen is asking, will Catherine prove to be a heroine?

Like Jane Austen herself, Catherine Morland has grown up in a rectory in a country village, in a large, happy, and secure family. In her teens she has become a great reader but, unlike Jane Austen and Fanny Price, the later heroine of *Mansfield Park*, Catherine has no one to guide her reading, and in recent years she has indulged in an unrestricted diet of Gothic novels, which have very much captured her imagination but have had a detrimental effect on her ability to be rational. At the age of seventeen Catherine leaves her family to spend a while with family friends, Mr and Mrs Allen, in Bath; and from there she goes to stay for a few weeks at Northanger Abbey, the home of the Tilney family, whom she has met in Bath. In these new settings, a long way away from her family and home, surrounded by new acquaintances, Catherine's character and values are tested.

In the first half of the novel she meets two families, the Thorpes and the Tilneys, who have very different values. She is immediately drawn to Isabella Thorpe, through both loneliness and a shared love of Gothic novels, and the two become friends. Catherine soon meets Isabella's brother John, who is a friend of her own brother James. Though James and Isabella become attached to each other, Catherine resists the emotional pressure of John Thorpe – about which Jane Austen comments: "[W]here youth and diffidence are united, it requires uncommon steadiness of mind to resist the attraction of being called the most charming girl in the world, and of being so very early engaged as a partner…" Even though he is James' friend and Isabella's brother, and she is thus under pressure to like him, Catherine finds John Thorpe's manners displeasing, and from his behaviour and his attitudes she begins to discern that his character is unsteady. Also, as the weeks in Bath progress, she becomes aware of Isabella's fickleness. For, despite her claim that "[o]f all things in the world inconstancy is my aversion", and her supposed attachment to James, Catherine can see that her friend still eagerly follows other young men around Bath, and shows an inappropriate interest in Captain Frederick Tilney.

Catherine has befriended other members of the Tilney family – Frederick's siblings, Henry and Eleanor. They are sensible and well-bred, and bring out the best in Catherine. She realizes that she enjoys their company more than that of the Thorpes:

> *It was no effort to Catherine to believe that Henry Tilney could never be wrong. His manner might sometimes surprize, but his meaning must always be just; and what she did not understand, she was almost as ready to admire, as what she did. The whole walk was delightful … The morning had passed away so charmingly as to banish all her friendship and natural affection; for no thought of Isabella or James crossed her mind during their walk.*

However, her promises to meet the Tilneys have been twice broken by the Thorpes' last-minute plans for excursions, for which John insists upon Catherine's company in his new two-seater gig. One of these excursions is an overambitious plan to drive to Blaize Castle, beyond Bristol, which John Thorpe commandingly describes as being "the oldest castle in the kingdom" but which is, as the readers of Jane Austen's day would have known, a sham contemporary edifice, built as a folly. This highlights the choice Catherine must make between allying herself with the Tilneys, with their traditional values of keeping promises, or with the fast, modern Thorpes, represented by Isabella's fickleness and John Thorpe's flash new gig, his fast talking, and his lack of concern for Catherine's reputation. Catherine chooses the Tilneys over the Thorpes, and is rewarded by being invited to stay at Northanger Abbey with Henry, Eleanor, and their father, General Tilney.

The second part of *Northanger Abbey* puts Catherine again in a new situation, this time in a former abbey, which excites all her romantic imaginings, sown by her unquestioning and unregulated reading of Gothic novels. She has looked forward in eager anticipation to Northanger's "massy walls of grey stone, rising amidst a grove of ancient oaks, with the last beams of the sun playing in beautiful splendour on its high Gothic windows". So initially she is disappointed by the house's modern appearance, but on her first night all her sensibilities are disturbed by the discovery of an old chest in her room, a mysterious bundle of papers, and along with them a violent gust of wind. The author parodies those same Gothic novels as we read that Catherine

trembled from head to foot. In the pause which succeeded, a sound like receding footsteps and the closing of a distant door struck on her affrighted ear. Human nature could support no more. A cold sweat stood on her forehead, the manuscript fell from her hand,

and groping her way to the bed, she jumped hastily in, and sought some suspension of agony by creeping far underneath the clothes. To close her eyes in sleep that night, she felt must be entirely out of the question.

But Catherine does sleep. In the morning she discovers the papers are only laundry bills and she chastises herself for her reaction. But her imagination does not entirely lose its hold on her, and she becomes convinced that the General's rather unpredictable behaviour (which she perceives as having "the air and attitude of a Montoni!" – Montoni being the villain of Mrs Radcliffe's *The Mysteries of Udolpho*) – is a sign of guilt over his cruelty to his wife, who died a number of years before. Catherine takes herself to Mrs Tilney's bedroom, where she is surprised by Henry who, to her shame, has discerned her suspicions:

If I understand you rightly, you had formed a surmise of such horror as I have hardly words to – Dear Miss Morland, consider the dreadful nature of the suspicions you have entertained. What have you been judging from? Remember the country and the age in which we live. Remember that we are English, that we are Christians. Consult your own understanding, your own sense of the probable, your own observation of what is passing around you – Does our education prepare us for such atrocities... Dearest Miss Morland, what ideas have you been admitting?"

Catherine has been recalled to common sense and the values of her upbringing. She needs to develop the virtue of prudence. The fantasies of the Gothic novel are in danger of corrupting the goodness of her nature, and have already undermined her capacity to form rational judgments. Catherine takes Henry's opinions to heart, for by the next morning she has realized

[c]harming as were all Mrs. Radcliffe's works, and charming
even as were the works of all her imitators, it was not in them
perhaps that human nature, at least in the midland counties
of England, was to be looked for... Among the Alps and the
Pyrenees, perhaps, there were no mixed characters. There, such
as were not spotless as an angel, might have the dispositions of
a fiend. But in England it was not so; among the English, she
believed, in their hearts and habits, there was a general though
unequal mixture of good and bad.

Catherine's folly is not in reading Gothic novels. The fact
that Henry also enjoys reading the Gothic genre, and indeed
has earlier told Catherine that he had been so gripped when
reading *The Mysteries of Udolpho* that he could not put it down,
shows that Jane Austen is not writing a polemic against the
Gothic novel as such. What Catherine is criticized for is reading
without thought or reflection, reading with too much sensibility
and not enough sense, and imposing the values of such novels
on her life and the lives of those around her. She needs to learn
to read with more detachment and criticism, and to balance the
reading of such novels with more serious books, especially on
history. For, in life and in literature, imagination must be ruled
by judgment; and other people's natures are to be critiqued
with a grounded realism.

The General abruptly demands that Catherine should
leave Northanger Abbey immediately, and she returns home,
convinced that she has lost all hope of Henry's love and respect.
The General's fickle behaviour is then explained: in Bath he had
been wrongly informed, by John Thorpe, that Catherine would
one day be a rich woman, after inheriting Mr Allen's fortune.
This had made him favour her as a future wife for Henry. His
rage on learning that he had been misinformed leads him to
throw Catherine out of Northanger Abbey. Henry follows her to

her home and assures her of his love. In time Eleanor becomes engaged to a rich man, and, with the future of Northanger secured through Eleanor's match, Henry is given his father's blessing to marry Catherine.

Jane Austen begins *Northanger Abbey* by querying what sort of heroine Catherine Morland might be. At the end of the novel she gives Catherine a heroine's reward, for she marries for love. Whilst not fulfilling the criteria for the heroine of a Gothic or Romantic Sentimental novel, for she has not faced or overcome any physical danger, she has faced and overcome great moral danger, so it is in the spiritual sense that Catherine emerges as a heroine in her author's eyes. On her own, away from home for the first time, amid all the temptations of Bath, Catherine has recognized the moral worth and chosen the friendship and the values of Henry and Eleanor Tilney over and against being drawn into the deceits and wiles of the materialistic John and Isabella Thorpe. She has come to recognize the dangers of an uncritical and unrestricted reading of Gothic and Romantic Sentimental novels, and has learned to curb her over-romantic imagination and become more prudent. In her self-examination and reflection, in her discernment between good character and bad, and in the growth of her own character, she has shown herself to be a true heroine in the understanding of her author, and so Jane Austen rewards her with marriage to the man she has come to love: "Henry and Catherine were married, the bells rang and everybody smiled…"

We have seen that each of Jane Austen's first three novels ends with a wedding for her main heroine or heroines – Elinor and Marianne Dashwood in *Sense and Sensibility*, Elizabeth and Jane Bennet in *Pride and Prejudice*, and Catherine Morland in *Northanger Abbey*. The wedding at the end of the story is not what each novel is essentially about: the greatest triumph of each book is the change that happens in the minds and hearts of her heroines (and sometimes her heroes), as they become the people they need to be in order to live good lives in their communities. Those characters who make such a change in their lives are rewarded with a happy marriage. Jane Austen's novels have been criticized for a lack of action, but I would argue that a huge amount happens in them – but principally in people's heads and hearts. Her heroes and heroines come to think seriously about how they live their lives, recognize what constitutes bad living and good living and, in the course of time, change their habits and develop virtues.

In these three early novels, each conceived and written as a first draft in Steventon Rectory, Jane Austen writes with great spiritual depth as she explores the place of values and character development leading to acquiring virtues; the possibility of life lived beyond materialism, where other things matter beyond what can be seen, touched, or acquired; and the importance of inner reflection. In the last of these novels, *Northanger Abbey*, Jane sends her leading character, Catherine, away from home to Bath, where the values and character formed by her upbringing in a country rectory are challenged and tested. Ironically, Jane Austen herself would now face that same challenge and testing in the city of Bath.

CHAPTER FOUR

THE WILDERNESS YEARS, 1801–09

"Wilderness"

In 1801, Jane Austen's happy and secure life at Steventon Rectory came to an unexpected and abrupt end. For the next eight years, her life changed drastically. Calling this period "the wilderness years" is to employ a biblical metaphor. The wilderness in the Bible is the rocky desert that forms part of Israel, and much of the land in the countries that surround it. In the Old Testament the people of Israel, on their escape from slavery in Egypt, spent forty years "wandering in the wilderness", before they were finally able to cross the Jordan River and enter the "Promised Land" of Canaan. It was in the wilderness that they received from God, through the prophet Moses, the laws by which they were to establish the nation of Israel in their new land, and by which they were to live their lives there in obedience to God. It was also during their time in the wilderness that they learned to trust God for all that they needed to survive, through his provision of water, quail, and manna – the bread-like substance that came only in the early morning with the dew. In the New Testament, Jesus Christ is driven out into the wilderness, where he is tempted by the devil to renounce his trust and dependence on God; but Christ withstands the temptations and returns from the wilderness with his sense of calling renewed. Jane Austen's "wilderness years" therefore refer to a barren and testing period of life – but not to years that were wasted. For Jane learned much from her understanding of the disappointment and loss that she experienced during these years – an understanding that was to be crucial to her later novels. And, when these years were over, she returned, renewed and re-energized, to her calling as a writer.

Jane would have been familiar with the use of the word "wilderness" in contemporary society for, as she was to depict in Sotherton in *Mansfield Park*, it was the fashion to have a wilderness area in the grounds of great houses. This was an area of land that was left uncultivated – it was often a place of bushy woodland, and served as a stark contrast to the highly managed and formally laid-out garden areas. For many people a wilderness provided a place of freedom and privacy, where the formal rules of social etiquette could for a short while be held in abeyance. For the first twenty-five years of her life, Jane had been "the Rector's younger daughter" – this had given her privilege and status within the neighbourhood of Steventon, but it also placed her within a tight framework of expectations and social rules. Leaving Steventon Rectory and moving to Bath were to give her a much greater freedom from the norms of behaviour in a country village.

The City of Bath

It was the Romans who first realized the potential of the hot springs that bubble up in the valley of the River Avon. Their engineers drained the land and built a city that covered twenty-three acres, which they named Aquae Sulis, meaning "the waters of Sulis" – Sulis being the Celtic goddess of health and healing. The Roman city soon became an international medical and religious centre, famed for its extensive system of baths. When the Romans left, the city was all but abandoned, until it became a place of national importance again in 973 when the coronation of King Edgar, the first king of all England, took place in the Saxon church that stood where Bath Abbey now stands. The developing wool business, creating a busy and lucrative trade in cloth between Britain and Europe, brought prosperity to Bath, which soon developed into a flourishing medieval town.

In 1702, shortly after her coronation, Queen Anne came to Bath seeking a cure for her gout. On her visit she performed the ceremony of "touching for the King's Evil": thirty poor people suffering from scrofula were touched on the neck by the Queen, in the belief that a cure would follow. She was the last English monarch to perform this ceremony. Her gout, unfortunately, was not alleviated, but there can be no doubt that her patronage of Bath was chiefly responsible for the remarkable increase in the number of fashionable visitors to the city during the years that followed. "Taking the waters" consisted of both drinking the warm water and bathing in it. For some people, their health was their main reason for coming to Bath; for others, though, as Bath became the vogue resort of the Georgian world, "taking the waters" became the pretext for coming to socialize and take part in the many fashionable entertainments that Bath offered.

Three different figures had brought Bath to the great prominence and fashion that it enjoyed in the eighteenth century: Ralph Allen, Beau Nash, and John Wood. The entrepreneur and philanthropist Ralph Allen, who began his working life as a Post Office clerk, worked his way up through the postal service to become Postmaster of Bath, and was made the city's Lord Mayor in 1742. With his newly acquired wealth he bought some nearby stone quarries, from which his new mansion, Prior Park, was built, which set the tone for the rebuilding of the city in the distinctive honey-coloured Bath stone that became its trademark.

Richard Nash, commonly known as Beau Nash, became Master of Ceremonies at Bath in 1704, a position he held for over fifty years. His position was unofficial, but nevertheless he had extensive influence in the city and far beyond. His role included meeting new arrivals to Bath, and judging whether they were suitable to join the select "company" of the five hundred or so people who had booked tables and had introductions brokered for them. Although the Allens and Catherine Morland came to the city after the era of Beau Nash, it can still be seen in *Northanger Abbey* that newcomers to Bath could not socialize at evening functions until they had been introduced by the Master of Ceremonies. After a lonely first evening engagement at the Upper Rooms, where they were ignored by the company, Mrs Allen and Catherine had a more successful second evening:

> *They made their appearance in the Lower Rooms; and here fortune was more favourable to our heroine. The master of the ceremonies introduced to her a very gentlemanlike young man as a partner; – his name was Tilney.*

Beau Nash was particularly notable for encouraging a new informality in manners by breaking down the rigid barriers that had previously divided the nobility and gentry from the middle-class patrons of Bath – once, of course, they had won the favour of the Master of Ceremonies. This gave Bath a sense of freedom and progressiveness that drew new residents and visitors in great numbers, eager to mix with people whom they would not be able to meet socially in their own neighbourhood.

John Wood, often known as John Wood the Elder, was the self-educated son of a Bath builder, who created an ambitious master plan for his home town in 1725. Fuelled by his passions for Palladianism (a type of classical architecture) and ancient

British history, Wood set out to restore Bath to what he believed was its former ancient glory as one of the most important and significant cities in England. Extraordinarily, he received his first break from a forbear of Jane Austen. As we have seen, one of Jane's maternal great-grandmothers had a sister who was married to James Brydges, the first Duke of Chandos, and it was he who gave the twenty-two-year-old John Wood the commission to build Chandos Buildings, a row of houses which are now part of Westgate Buildings. Though that was the Duke's only commission in Bath, Chandos Buildings led to more commissions for John Wood and launched his career, enabling him to fulfil many of the aspirations of his master plan. After opposition from the Freemen and Corporation, his main developments had to be built outside the existing walls of the medieval city. His most famous developments included Queen Square and The Circus and, on the other side of the old city, North and South Parades, all made up of distinctive five-storeyed houses with pediments and friezes built of the local Bath stone. Thus Wood created a distinctive image for the city.

His son, often known as John Wood the Younger, continued his father's style, and his works included the Royal Crescent and the Assembly Rooms (known in Jane Austen's novels as the Upper Rooms). Following Wood the Younger, who died in 1782, there were plenty more philanthropists and builders such as Robert Adam, who designed Pulteney Bridge, and Sir William Pulteney, who commissioned Great Pulteney Street. They and others continued to develop Bath in the style set by John Wood, for the ever-growing numbers of people wanting to come to live or stay in this progressive city – including, in 1801, Revd and Mrs George Austen with their two daughters, Cassandra and Jane.

Hearing the News

In December 1800, Jane and Cassandra were both away from home. Jane was staying with her close friend Martha Lloyd at Ibthorpe, twenty miles from Steventon, and Cassandra was with their brother Edward at his Godmersham estate in Kent, helping the family out during the arrival of a sixth baby. With no consultation with any of their children, Revd and Mrs Austen made the decision to retire from the parishes, putting their son James in as curate, and move to Bath. Jane was told the news as she walked in through the door on her return home, and the family story is that the shock was so great that she fainted. Most of the family furniture and books were to be sold – the rest, including all the pictures, were to be left to James and his family, who were eager to move into the Rectory.

Cassandra was still in away Kent when Jane returned. No doubt Jane would have written to her sister to break the news and tell of her own reaction, but no letters to Cassandra survive from that month.[1] In later life, as Jane became more famous and it became clear that people outside the family circle would want to read her correspondence, Cassandra destroyed[2] any letters in which Jane expressed emotions that she felt were too raw to be seen by others' eyes. The few letters from this time that did survive Cassandra's cull show that Jane had no real enthusiasm for Bath. She had enjoyed Bath as a visitor, but she had no desire to live there, though she was glad to be nearer to Wales and to English seaside resorts for holidays.

In May 1801 Jane and her mother travelled to Bath to stay with the Leigh-Perrots at The Paragon on Walcot Street while they looked for a house to rent. This was a dispiriting process for, although a number of houses were viewed, many were out of their price range, and others were unsuitable because the rooms were too small or, as in the case of possible rooms in

Green Park Buildings, considered to be too damp. In the end the family settled in a very favourably placed house in Sydney Place, at the end of the recently finished Pulteney Street and opposite the fashionable Sydney Gardens. Jane had originally thought that the rents in this part of Bath were too high, but the house was cheaper than expected because they got it part-way through the lease.

The Austens did not move into their new home until the autumn of 1801, and spent much of the summer on a prolonged holiday in Devon, before visiting family and friends in Hampshire. The family had received an invitation from Jane's cousin, Revd Edward Cooper, rector of Hamstall Ridware in Staffordshire, to stay with him: "Edward Cooper is so kind as to want us all to come to Hamstall this summer, instead of going to the sea, but we are not so kind as to mean to do it,"[3] Jane had written to Cassandra earlier in the year. Edward, who was four years older than Jane Austen, and his sister Jane had spent a lot of time with their Austen cousins throughout their childhoods. As we have seen, Jane Cooper had been the companion of Cassandra and Jane in their school years, but had been killed three years previously when a runaway dray horse had careered into the gig she was driving.

Relations between Jane Austen and Edward were strained, as is suggested by Jane's private comment to Cassandra on hearing that Edward had accepted the Hamstall living and was moving from Oxfordshire: "We collect from his letter that he means to reside there, in which he shows his wisdom. Staffordshire is a good way off..."[4] Jane found Edward too serious-minded and pompous, and the two of them must have had words on the matter, for when a new Cooper baby was born just as the Austens were preparing to move to Bath, Jane writes to Cassandra: "I have heard twice from Edward on the occasion, and his letters have each been exactly what they ought to be – cheerful and amusing.

He dares not write otherwise to *me*, but perhaps he might be obliged to purge himself from the guilt of writing nonsense by filling his shoes with whole peas for a week afterwards."[5]

The Bath Years

Sadly, no letters written by Jane between June 1801 and January 1805 are still in existence, except one from an 1804 holiday in Lyme Regis. This may be because she and Cassandra were always together, though that is unlikely, as Cassandra was increasingly called upon to stay with Edward's family in Kent, particularly during his wife's many confinements. It is much more likely that there were letters from this period, but Cassandra destroyed them. For the Bath years were not happy ones for Jane. A description sent to Cassandra of the view of Bath from the top of Kingsdown Hill on Jane's arrival for their house-hunting visit in May 1801 seems to set the tone for the years ahead:

> *The first view of Bath in fine weather does not answer my expectations; I think I see more distinctly through rain. The sun was got behind everything, and the appearance of the place from the top of Kingsdown was all vapour, shadow, smoke, and confusion.*[6]

The Bath that she had described in *Northanger Abbey* reflects the visits Jane had made there when she was a young woman in 1797 and 1799 when, like young Catherine Morland, she was all wide-eyed wonder. It was to be a very different experience to live in the place full-time, when she was in her mid to late twenties, with no happy Steventon Rectory to return to at the end of a short stay away. Jane Austen's Bath experience now was much more akin to that of the older Anne Elliot in her later novel *Persuasion*, in which Jane refers to "the white glare of Bath". This is a city of empty socializing, name dropping, and desire for social climbing, and Anne persists "in a very determined, though very silent, disinclination for Bath…"

A wide variety of public entertainment was on offer to the Austen family – though the correspondence that we have makes it clear that they felt restricted in what they could take part in, by their limited financial means. In a typical week at the beginning of the nineteenth century, residents and visitors could attend a number of balls in two different venues, the Upper Rooms and the Lower Rooms, with a room set aside for card playing for those like Mr Allen of *Northanger Abbey* who were not inclined to dance. There were regular concerts and choral works in the Rooms and, each week, three performances at the theatre – a larger theatre was built and opened during the Austens' residency. It was the fashion to go to the Pump Rooms in the morning, to drink the waters, and to watch people and be watched by them. Some people bathed in the public baths at least once a day. The Sydney Pleasure Gardens, opposite the Austens' first home in Sydney Place, offered public breakfasts and evening concerts, often with fireworks. Yet although Jane Austen in her Steventon days had expressed a great fondness for dancing, for play-acting, and for music, she had much less enthusiasm for taking part in these activities in Bath:

> *There is to be a grand gala on Tuesday evening in Sydney Gardens, a concert, with illuminations and fireworks. To the latter Elizabeth and I look forward with pleasure, and even the concert will have more than its usual charm for me, as the gardens are large enough for me to get pretty well beyond the reach of its sound.*[7]

Bath had itself changed between Jane's teenage visits and her residence a few years later, for the royal family were changing their allegiance from Bath to Brighton, making Bath less popular than it had been in the last decades of the eighteenth century. This led to a greater competitiveness to meet the socially superior people who were there. Previously the focus of society had been on balls and concerts at the Assembly Rooms, which were open to everyone, but in the early 1800s this was beginning to change to a preference for more select private parties in homes. Jane did not much enjoy these smaller parties, which enforced longer conversations with people whom she often found tedious. In writing to Cassandra from the house-hunting visit before their move, Jane writes of "[a]nother stupid party last night; perhaps if larger they might be less intolerable";[8] and she wrote of people who "talk nonsense to each other" and "I cannot anyhow continue to find people agreeable…" Later, however, she did go to a party that was "not quite so stupid as the two preceding parties here".[9]

The change from large public gatherings to smaller private parties led to a sense of pressure to be invited to the right parties, which in turn led to the greater ostentation and snobbery that we see illustrated in Sir Walter Elliot's fawning behaviour towards his social superior, Lady Dalrymple, in *Persuasion*. His preference for select gatherings also made it harder for Anne to meet Captain Wentworth, for

> *[t]he theatre, or the rooms, where he was most likely to be, were not fashionable enough for the Elliots, whose evening amusements were solely in the elegant stupidity of private parties, in which they were getting more and more engaged; and Anne… was quite impatient for the concert evening. It was a concert for the benefit of a person patronised by Lady Dalrymple. Of course they must attend. It was really expected to be a good one, and Captain Wentworth was very fond of music.*

It is surely not by chance that Jane Austen set Sir Walter Elliot's Bath lodging in Camden Crescent, which had been ambitiously built in such a steep location that two of its houses had fallen down, making the Crescent off balance. Camden Crescent thus serves as a metaphor for Sir Walter's precarious life, for he continues to live beyond his means and with unrealistic social ambition. The off-balance Camden Crescent is perhaps also a statement of how Jane Austen saw Bath.

Jane was developing the virtues that would form such an intrinsic part of her later novels – constancy, faithfulness, and integrity. She did not see these virtues reflected in the society around her in Bath. Her comments from the letters that we have suggest that the constant seeking after pleasure in the endless round of social activities struck her as lacking purpose and serious intent; and that the constant desire to impress others seemed vain and affected to her. Today we see the Bath of Jane Austen's day through a romantic, historical lens but, for her, the city still being built around her was a new development, the buildings themselves often reflecting the fickleness of the society she was experiencing. In Sydney Place, as she watched new streets of buildings being so hastily built, she would have seen the splendour of the highly decorated and elegant façades, but she would have been aware of the cheapness of the stone and the shoddiness of the workmanship at the back of the houses. Bath did not reflect the values and the virtues that she cherished. She could find little depth in the superficial and materialistic life lived by so many people around her. It is not surprising that she was often unhappy living there.

Though she would have known Bath Abbey (then, as today, the most famous church in Bath), the family mainly worshipped in proprietary chapels, including St Mary's Chapel on Queen Square and Laura Chapel, just off Laura Place, which was the nearest place of Anglican worship to Sydney

Place. Proprietary chapels were built to serve the needs of the rapidly expanding, though often seasonal, population of Bath, before more substantial parish churches could be built. Laura Chapel was built to seat a thousand worshippers. St Mary the Virgin Church, Bathwick, which served the new parish around Pulteney Street and Sydney Gardens, was not consecrated until 1820. So, during these Bath years, Jane was worshipping in churches that had no feel of history or rootedness in the community. She was accustomed to worshipping in settled parish churches, where she both knew and was known by her fellow worshippers and the service was led by someone she knew, so she was used to being "on the inside" of what was going on in the life of the church. Consequently, Sunday church worship, though the service would follow the Prayer Book format she had always known, may have been another lonely and unfamiliar experience for her.

Jane must also have had a sense of being on the marriage market – for Mr and Mrs Austen moved to Bath with unmarried daughters aged twenty-eight and twenty-five, and Bath was seen by many as an obvious place to come to find a husband for unmarried daughters. Jane's parents themselves had got married there and may even have met there (though it is possible, as we have seen, that they were already acquainted in Oxford). Jane would also have been aware that her aunt Philadelphia, her father's sister, had once been on the marriage market, for she had been sent to India to find a husband. There is perhaps a hint of this awareness of the expectations weighing on her in her words to Cassandra from the house-hunting trip: "I am prevented from setting my black cap at Mr Maitland by his having a wife & ten children."[10]

It seems that there was a significant romantic encounter for Jane, however, but the details are very sketchy, as it was mentioned only in passing by Cassandra to her niece Caroline many years after the event.[11] On one of the Austen family holidays during the Bath years, most probably during the summer of 1802, the family were staying in Devon for a few weeks and Jane met a young man, in whom, Cassandra felt, she had shown the beginnings of a romantic interest. When they parted, after having met and talked often over a period of a few weeks, they agreed to meet again, but soon afterwards news reached the Austens that he had died. There was another passed-down family story[12] of greater reliability, that during the autumn of 1802, after the family had gone back to Bath, Jane and Cassandra went on a long visit to friends and family, and stayed for a few days with their old Hampshire friends the Bigg sisters at Manydown House, near to their old home in Steventon. Encouraged by his sisters, their younger brother, Harris Bigg-Wither, who was five years younger than Jane, proposed to her one evening. Jane accepted, to the delight of the whole household. However, after lying awake for many hours through the night, she asked to see him again the next morning and told him that, while she esteemed and respected him, she did not love him, and so she needed to turn down his proposal. Maybe, at twenty-seven, she had initially grasped with relief what she thought might be her last opportunity to be married, along with the opportunity it gave her to live in Hampshire again, but had realized in the night that it was better to remain unmarried than to enter a marriage that she believed she might soon regret.

Jane was lonely in Bath. In her Hampshire days she had formed very close friendships with women both of her own age and older than her. During one of her many long stays in Kent, Cassandra wrote encouraging her to make new friends in Bath, suggesting in particular a Mrs Chamberlayne. "I respect Mrs. Chamberlayne for doing her hair well, but cannot feel a more tender sentiment,"[13] was Jane's response. She did often go walking and visiting with Mrs Chamberlayne but they seem to have remained just acquaintances. By the nature of the society of Bath, people came and went, which added to the difficulty of making friends, and perhaps those who came to Bath by their own choice would as a consequence have a very different approach to life and different values from Jane, so they would have little in common. So, although she formed acquaintances, no close friends like those from her Steventon days were to emerge from this period in her life. It seems that Jane Austen did not relish the greater social freedoms that living in Bath gave her, but rather missed the more ordered and structured society of village life. Perhaps this is not surprising, for in Steventon she had grown up forming relationships through her father's parish duties and his farming, relationships which were deeply embedded in a rooted community and in her family's position in society. This is suggested in a letter to Cassandra written in April 1805, in which she refers to another member of the Chamberlayne family:

This morning we have been to see Miss Chamberlayne look hot on horseback. – Seven years & four months ago we went to the same Ridinghouse to see Miss Lefroy's performance! – What a different set we are now moving in![14]

Miss Lefroy was Lucy, the daughter of Anne Lefroy, Jane's great friend and near neighbour from Steventon.

Mrs Chamberlayne did, however, provide a helpful service to Jane in being a walking companion. Bath, like Rome, is built on seven hills and, for a keen and fit walker like Jane, there was much pleasure to be had in walking out of the city to nearby villages among the surrounding hills. On an earlier visit with her family in 1799, Jane had written of walks to Weston and Charlcombe, which she had clearly very much enjoyed, and in letters that we have from 1801 we hear of walks to Weston and in the Lyncombe and Widcombe valleys with Mrs Chamberlayne, who was an energetic and intrepid walker:

In climbing a hill Mrs Chamberlayne is very capital; I would with difficulty keep pace with her, yet would not flinch for the world. On plain ground I was quite her equal. And so we posted away under a hot sun, **she** *without any parasol or shade to her hat, stopping for nothing...*[15]

The lack of letters from her Bath years means we do not know how much Jane was able to indulge in the walks around the city that were such a great pleasure to her. She had once clarified to Cassandra that it was the physical act of walking that she found life-giving, not just the delight of the views at the culmination of the walk.[16] We do hear in 1805 of some walks along canals, and on one occasion a trip was proposed to "the Cassoon" – probably a reference to a lift (caisson lock) on the Somerset Coal Canal at Combe Hay.

Although Bath is built on seven hills, much of the city, and all of the different houses in which the Austens stayed, are in a bowl, which can feel oppressive, especially on hot summer days. The nearby River Avon caused some houses to be damp, as Jane knew from some of those she had visited when house hunting, and no doubt the river and nearby canal could be very smelly at times. In her novel *Mansfield Park*, written eight years after she had left Bath, Jane reflects on how Fanny, who has lived in the countryside for the last few years, finds living in the town of Portsmouth:

She felt that she had, indeed, been three months there; and the sun's rays falling strongly into the parlour, instead of cheering, made her still more melancholy; for sunshine appeared to her a totally different thing in a town and in the country. Here, its power was only a glare, a stifling, sticky glare, serving but to

bring forward stains and dirt that might otherwise have slept.
There was neither health nor gaiety in sunshine in a town.

One wonders if the country-loving Jane Austen is reflecting on her own experience of living in the town of Bath in these words. Certainly it is interesting to note that for Catherine in *Northanger Abbey*, for whom staying in Bath was a broadly happy experience, walks and drives out into the countryside play a large part. Catherine is introduced to walking by the Tilneys, keen walkers themselves, and is taken up Beechen Cliff by them to see the view of the city. But Jane Austen portrays the morally lax Isabella and John Thorpe as having no interest in or understanding of the benefits and delights of walking. Instead, they drive everywhere at the greatest speed possible – John Thorpe in the gig he has just bought on the cheap from a fellow student, but which he believes to be the height of fashion.

Anne Elliot of *Persuasion* loves a country walk, as we see from her eagerness for walks around Uppercross and Lyme. Unfortunately, Anne, whose experience of Bath is one of restriction, is further hampered by never being able to get out of the city. The propriety of her day meant that she could not take a walk alone, and her only companions are Mrs Smith, who is disabled and unable to leave her home, and Lady Russell, who sees walking as beneath her dignity and goes everywhere in her carriage. Yet Anne's walks through the city are recorded with such local detail by Jane Austen that one senses that, in this respect at least, Jane is remembering Bath with some fondness.

The Austen family were often away for long stretches at a time during the Bath years, either at the seaside or staying with friends. Though Jane looked forward to these visits, they were not conducive to writing, for she needed a settled environment in which to do that. The one letter in existence from this time is written from Lyme Regis in 1804, providing evidence that, when

Jane later in life described the resort with its striking Cobb jutting out into the sea in *Persuasion*, she was writing from experience. Perhaps the idea of her future unfinished novel *Sanditon*, set in a developing seaside resort, was born during these family visits to increasingly fashionable seaside places during the early years of the nineteenth century.

There are frequent references to money in the letters that we have from this period – relief that some food items were cheaper in Bath than they were in the Hampshire countryside, and concern about the cost of other things. Given that the housekeeping seemed to fall mainly to Jane, it seems that she carried quite a lot of responsibility for the economic well-being of the family. There would have been no clergy pension for the Austen family. Their only income would have been the tithes paid to her father, who remained the rector of Steventon and Deane until he died, though he had been able to raise the tithe by a little before he left. However, a proportion of this income needed to be paid to James, as curate. Jane would know that the income from the tithes would cease immediately on her father's death.

During 1802 or 1803 Jane Austen picked up her 1799 manuscript *Susan* again – this was the work that eventually became *Northanger Abbey*, and much of it was set in Bath. She drafted a second copy and, in the spring of 1803, a business partner of her brother Henry sold it to a London publisher, Crosby & Co., for £10, on the understanding that it would be published. This must have given Jane encouragement, for soon afterwards she managed to begin a novel of great promise, *The Watsons*, completing about seventeen and a half thousand words. But the novel was abandoned, and there is no evidence that she ever returned to it. In the bustling environment of Bath, with the financial responsibilities and worries Jane shouldered, it was difficult for her to find the calm and quiet space in her mind that she needed for reflection and creativity. However, Jane's nephew James Austen-Leigh later suggested that Jane abandoned the work because she regretted placing her heroine in too lowly a situation.[17] The heroine of this novel, Emma Watson, comes from the poorest of all of Jane's leading families – they ate their dinner off a tray and the family worried about domestic matters such as the cost of washing day. The Watson family were, economically speaking, in a similar situation to Jane's own family. However, it is very likely that writing *The Watsons* also became too difficult because Emma's situation became too much like Jane's in another way. For Emma Watson is about to become an orphan and, just a few months into writing the novel, Jane suffered a double bereavement: in December 1804, her closest friend from her Steventon days, Anne Lefroy, died in a riding accident, and in January 1805, Jane's beloved father died after a very quick final illness.

It was a peaceful death. As Jane wrote to her brother Frank, "Our dear Father has closed his virtuous & happy life, in a death almost as free from suffering as his Children could have wished."[18] Jane had loved her father dearly, and she describes his corpse as preserving "the sweet, benevolent smile which always distinguished him".[19] Though she keeps up a cheerful front in subsequent letters, Jane must have grieved a great deal. Not only had Revd George Austen always been a loving father to her, he had greatly encouraged her reading and writing, so much so that he had tried to get her novel *First Impressions* published when she was only twenty-one. Jane had had a much deeper bond with her father than she had with her mother. With her father's death she could no longer be influenced and inspired by his values, his character, and his faith – all of which she had so much respected and admired.

The family by this stage had left Sydney Place, perhaps for reasons of economy rather than by choice, as they moved to Green Park Buildings – to one of the damp, "putrefying houses" that Jane had rejected four years earlier. Now they had no income from the parishes of Steventon and Deane. By April 1805, three months after Mr Austen's death, the Austen women had moved again and were living in Gay Street, having had to downsize again in terms of both rent and domestic help, although the brothers clubbed together to support them. Cassandra had a yearly income from the legacy left to her by her fiancé, but Jane had no private income of her own. After a long time away visiting family and friends in Kent and Hampshire, the Austen ladies found new temporary lodgings while looking for something more suitable. They were now in Trim Street, a location the family had previously done all in their power to avoid, for it was in one of the most distasteful parts of Bath, with noisy public houses, and was possibly in what we know today as a red-light area. However, a new plan emerged – for the family to move to Southampton to lodge with Frank's soon-to-be wife, Mary.

In July 1806 the Austens left Bath for good – two years later Jane was still remembering her "happy feelings of Escape!" After three months visiting family and friends in various parts of the country, they finally settled in Southampton in October 1807, initially in temporary lodgings before moving into a house on Castle Square in March 1807, with Jane's brother Frank and his new wife. He was home when the family arrived, but soon needed to return to sea for the next few years, and was grateful for his new bride, Mary, to have some company.

Living in Southampton

Jane now had a small legacy of £50 from one of her Aunt Leigh-Perrot's circle of Bath friends, which helped her through that first year in Southampton, but life was hard for her as she greatly missed her father and, as her frequent references to her mother's health in her letters suggest, was finding her mother more querulous and difficult as she got older.

Disappointingly, visits from her eldest brother James were not easy either. James had been the object of her greatest admiration as a child but now she wrote: "I am sorry and angry that his visits should not give one more pleasure; the company of so good and so clever a man ought to be gratifying in itself; but his chat seems all forced, his opinions on many points too much copied from his wife's, and his time here is spent I think in walking about the house and banging the doors."[20] Jane's long visits to family and friends continued, perhaps made longer by the difficulty for women of travelling alone. She always needed to wait for one of her brothers to be free to accompany her to her next destination.

Such an unsettled existence seems to have made it impossible for her to write, and there is no evidence from her correspondence or from later family recollections that Jane wrote anything other than letters during this period of her life. These letters contained as much news and gossip as ever, but they lacked the cutting or even playful wit of those from her Steventon days. In visits to and from friends and family, there seems much that led to dissatisfaction. There was disappointment from Crosby and Co., who had promised in 1803 to publish *Susan* but had not done so. In April 1809, Jane contacted them under the assumed name of "Mrs Ashton Dennis", offering to supply a second copy should the first have been lost, and saying she was prepared to send it to another publisher if they were no longer interested. She received a reply by return of post informing her that "… there was not any time stipulated for its publication, neither are we bound to publish it. Should you or anyone else we shall take proceedings to stop the sale. The MS shall be yours for the same as we paid for it."[21] Just two months later an anonymous novel also called *Susan* was published by another author – so

Jane knew that she would need to change both her heroine's name and the novel's title, if she ever wished to see the book published. It was not until 1816 that Jane finally paid Crosby and Co., and redeemed her manuscript.

There was another family bereavement in October 1808 when Edward's wife, Elizabeth, died very unexpectedly a fortnight after giving birth to her eleventh child. Jane was usually reticent about her Christian beliefs but at times of bereavement and crisis she wrote more openly of their importance. To Cassandra, she wrote of her brother Edward: "God be praised that you can say what you do of him: that he has a religious mind to bear him up, and a disposition that will gradually lead him to comfort," and she spoke of Elizabeth as having passed from "this world to a better".[22] It was important to her that Edward's oldest boys went to church when they came to stay with their aunts soon afterwards, and that they listened to and were affected by the sermon.[23]

Money concerns had returned, for Southampton rents were rising and, with Frank's own family now growing, the Austen women were beginning to feel that they were trespassing on Frank and Mary's hospitality and generosity. In the autumn of 1808, a move to Alton, the neighbouring town to Chawton, Jane's brother Edward's Hampshire estate, was being considered. But this all changed with the death of Elizabeth Knight, for, within a few days of her death, Edward, recognizing his need to have his wider family closer to his motherless children, wrote to his mother offering her and his sisters the choice of either a cottage near his Godmersham estate in Kent, or one on his Chawton estate. Chawton was the obvious choice. Despite the loss of her sister-in-law, Jane's spirits seem to have soared at this prospect, enabling her to enter energetically into the social life of Southampton for her remaining weeks there.

In July 1809 Jane Austen moved, with her mother and sister, to the seventeenth-century, six-bedroomed cottage in the village of Chawton, back in her beloved Hampshire and just fifteen miles from where she was born. This was the home in which she was to flourish. The eight long years in the wilderness were over.

CHAPTER FIVE

THE CHAWTON YEARS, 1809–16

The Return to her Writing

On moving to Chawton in July 1809, Jane settled down to work, serious in her determination to get her books published at last, despite the disappointment over *Susan* in April. First she turned to her teenage writings, her *Juvenilia*, and made some corrections and updates. Then she was ready to move on to the drafts of her first two novels. Throughout 1810, she prepared *Sense and Sensibility* for publication with a new publisher, Thomas Egerton of Whitehall, and in November 1811 Jane Austen at last held one of her published novels in her hand. It was not published under her own name, however, but was described as being by "a Lady". Meanwhile, she was redrafting *First Impressions*, changing the title to *Pride and Prejudice*.

Once she was a published author, Jane Austen continued to write. Her most concentrated writing happened when she was at home at Chawton, though visitors to the house often had no idea what Jane was producing. Her brother James' three children frequently stayed at the cottage and were unaware, at the time, that their aunt's writing, at the tiny table by the window in the dining room, was the composition of a novel and not merely the scrawling of letters to the family's many relatives. Many years later, one of these children, James Edward Austen-Leigh, wrote:

She was careful that her occupation should not be suspected
by servants, or visitors, or any persons beyond her own family
party. She wrote upon small sheets of paper which could easily
be put away, or covered with a piece of blotting paper. There
was, between the front door and the offices, a swing door which
creaked when it was opened; but she objected to having this little
inconvenience remedied, because it gave her notice when anyone
was coming... In that well-occupied female party there must have
been many precious hours of silence during which the pen was
busy at the little mahogany writing-desk, while Fanny Price, or
Emma Woodhouse, or Anne Elliot was growing into beauty and
interest. I have no doubt that I, and my sisters and cousins ...
frequently disturbed this mystic process, without having any idea
of the mischief we were doing; certainly we never should have
guessed it by any signs of impatience or irritability in the writer.[1]

Her ideas and inspiration did still flow, however, when she was on long visits away from home to friends and family. The "working", in this quote by one of Edward Knight's young daughters, refers to needlework of some sort, for Jane was a very gifted needlewoman:

Aunt Jane would sit quietly working beside the fire in the library,
saying nothing for a good while, and then would suddenly burst
out laughing, jump up and run across the room to a table where
pens and paper were lying, write something down and then come
back to the fire and go on working quietly as before.[2]

What a contrast between this focused activity and production of work during these first years at Chawton, and the previous unproductive eight years. Now we see the behaviour of a settled woman who is confident in her place in the world, who is indeed finding her voice. What has made such a change possible?

Jane was living again in a village, and one that was only a few miles from her birthplace. By returning to life in a village, she was back in a world in which she felt at home and knew where and how she fitted in. From her doorstep she could embark on the countryside walks that she so relished. After the peripatetic existence of the last eight years, she could be confident that she would be living in this house for many years. After staying with relatives or in rented houses on lease, the family were now in their own home; they could order their lives according to their own preferences and establish their own routines. This gave Jane more time for herself – for her mother took charge of the cottage garden with much enjoyment and no longer required Jane's company during the daytime, while Cassandra took responsibility for most of the housekeeping. Martha Lloyd, a close friend of Jane from her childhood days, was now living with the Austen family, and she took on many of the household duties, freeing Jane's time even more for her writing, as well as providing her with companionship in her times of leisure.

Jane was thirty-three when they moved back to Chawton, and it was now very unlikely that she would marry. No doubt that gave her some sense of loss, but perhaps there was also a sense of relief that there was no longer any burden of expectation upon her to marry. Being unmarried gave her the freedom to devote much more of her time and energy to her writing. She had been teased, however, by Mrs Knight, Edward's adopted mother, before the move to Chawton, about her marrying the bachelor vicar of Chawton, Revd John Papillon, but she responded with a show of lively wit: "I am very obliged to Mrs Knight for such a proof of the interest she takes in me, and she may depend upon it that I *will* marry Mr Papillon, whatever may be his reluctance or my own. I owe her much more than such a trifling sacrifice."[3] She clearly felt no awkwardness in

Mr Papillon's company, however, for she was a frequent guest at dinners and parties at the Chawton vicarage, though both Jane Austen and Mr Papillon remained unmarried throughout their lives.

With her return to village life, Jane was now a member of a village church again, and part of a congregation at Chawton church with whom she hoped she would be worshipping for many years to come. At social events at the vicarage she met and discussed church matters with many of the local clergy, and her letters from Chawton abound with reference to these men and their appointments. Jane was back in a world in which she felt at home.

With the success of *Sense and Sensibility* came not just the thrill of fulfilling her dream of being a published author, but also the relief of having some financial independence at last: "'Its' being sold will I hope be a great saving of Trouble to Henry, & therefore must be welcome to me," she wrote in a letter to Martha Lloyd after receiving the promise of £110 on the sale of her *Pride and Prejudice* manuscript to Thomas Egerton: "The Money is to be paid at the end of the twelvemonth."[4] At her death, however, it became apparent that she had saved most of her income against the possibility of more impecunious days ahead.

The wilderness years were not wasted ones for Jane Austen. While *Sense and Sensibility*, *Pride and Prejudice*, and *Northanger Abbey* sparkle with the confidence, high spirits, and hope of the young woman who created their first drafts in her teens and early twenties, into the later novels of *Mansfield Park*, *Emma*, and *Persuasion* she brought much of the maturity, wisdom, and life experience of those difficult eight years. She had not lost her playfulness or her love of the comic, but she no longer used these to critique the absurdities of literature as she had done in her *Juvenilia*, *Sense and Sensibility*, and *Northanger Abbey*. These gifts she now used primarily to satirize human absurdities, which served as a contrast to the challenges faced by the heroines of her later novels.

Her niece Anna commented:

> *Her unusually quick sense of the ridiculous inclined her to play with the trifling commonplaces of everyday life, whether as regarded people or things; but she never played with its serious duties or responsibilities – when she was grave she was **very** grave.*[5]

The Writings of Hannah More

In a letter to Cassandra written in January 1809, a few months before the move to Chawton, Jane responded to a comment, evidently made by Cassandra in her last letter, about a recently published novel by Mrs Hannah More, *Cœlebs in Search of a Wife*:

> *You have by no means raised my curiosity after Caleb. My disinclination for it before was affected, but now it is real. I do not like the evangelicals. Of course I shall be delighted when I read it, like other people, but till I do I dislike it.*[6]

Six days later, having been corrected by Cassandra about her mistake in the name of the leading character, she writes:

> *I am not at all ashamed about the name of the novel, having been guilty of no insult towards your handwriting; the diphthong I always saw, but knowing how fond you were of adding a vowel wherever you could, I attributed it to that alone, and the knowledge of the truth does the book no service; the only merit it could have was in the name of Caleb, which has an honest, un-pretending sound, but in Cœlebs there is pedantry and affectation.*[7]

Hannah More was an English religious writer and philanthropist. Born in Bristol in 1745, she taught at a school established by her father before opening a number of schools herself in some of the poorer villages in Somerset. She began her writing career by writing plays, and became involved with the literary elite in London. In time her plays and poetry became more evangelical and she became part of the Clapham Sect, who, under the leadership of the politician William Wilberforce, campaigned to end the transatlantic slave trade. In the 1790s, Hannah More wrote several tracts covering moral, religious, and political topics,[8] which were published widely, so, even before they heard about her novel *Cœlebs*, the Austen household would already have known Hannah More's name and reputation.

Cœlebs was Hannah More's only novel and was written with the express intention of encouraging her readers to emulate Cœlebs by converting to his form of evangelical Christianity. Jane was clearly not a fan of the evangelical or didactic novel, something she emphasized when revising her story *Catherine*, from her *Juvenilia*, in 1809. Catherine's aunt bestows some "pious literature" on her unappreciative niece to help to "breed her up virtuously", and, in the earlier version of the story, this was Bishop Seccar's explanation on the Catechism. However, Jane now replaced it with Hannah More's *Cœlebs in Search of a Wife*.

In his reflection on his sister's life, written in 1818, the year after her death, Henry Austen, who was by then ordained as an Anglican clergyman and a well-respected preacher himself, wrote:

> *She might defy the most fastidious critic to call any of her novels (as **Cœlebs** was designated) a dramatic sermon. The subject is rather alluded to, and that incidentally, than studiously brought*

forward and dwelt upon. In fact, she is more sparing of it than would be thought desirable by some persons; perhaps even by herself, had she consulted merely her own sentiments; but she probably introduced it as far as she thought would be generally profitable; for when the purpose of inculcating a religious principle is made too palpably prominent, many readers, if they do not throw aside the book with disgust, are apt to fortify themselves with that respectful kind of apathy with which they undergo a regular sermon, and prepare themselves as they do to swallow a dose of medicine, endeavouring to get it down in large gulps, without tasting it more than necessary.[9]

Henry believed that Jane was seeking to reflect her Christian faith in her novels, but that she did not believe that a didactic approach would be either popular or beneficial. A didactic novel aims to put forward one very particular point of view, and is written in an authoritarian tone for the express purpose of persuading the reader to adopt that point of view for themselves. A non-didactic novel is written not to make points but to entertain: to invent new worlds and invite the reader to pass the thresholds of their current existence and explore new ideas and experiences. It can be noted that Hannah More's didactic novel *Cœlebs* has sunk without trace whereas Jane Austen's novels continue to be read avidly by new generations, and have been continuously, ever since her death, now two hundred years ago.

So, if Jane Austen was not going to write to a set Christian agenda how, to quote Henry, did she "allude" to her Christian faith? In what ways did she "inculcate Christian principles", albeit in a discreet way? Many readers today read her novels without picking up any hints of her beliefs, but critics and biographers of the past have been in no doubt that this is a woman writing from a strongly Christian position. For example,

David Cecil, Professor of English Literature at the University of Oxford from 1948 to 1970, wrote in *A Portrait of Jane Austen*, published in 1978:

> *Jane Austen's religion, so her biographer discovers as he studies her, is an element in her life of the highest significance and importance. The Austen reticence kept her from ever talking much about it. But the little she did say, and what her intimates said about her, show that she grew up to be deeply religious. She actively practised her faith and her moral views were wholly, if unobtrusively, determined by the dictates of the Christian religion as interpreted by her church.*[10]

Before turning to the novels of Jane's Chawton years, which we will do in the next two chapters, we will look to see what clues we can discern from her personal religious practice, her letters, and her written prayers that help us to determine the nature of her spirituality.

Jane Austen's Religious Practice

We know from family testimony and from her letters that Jane attended Chawton church regularly, twice on a Sunday when both a morning and an evening service were held. If there was no evening service, or if the weather was too bad to go out, the Austen family would hold their own Sunday-evening prayers at home, which Jane led when Cassandra was away. A sermon was read from a book of sermons, and the frequent references to books of sermons in her letters show that Jane was a great reader and commentator on such writings.[11]

Jane had her own copy of *A Companion to the Altar* by William Vickers, a book written to be used in preparing for Holy Communion, a service which was held only occasionally in Jane Austen's day. Vickers' intention in this book is to "encourage religious reflection among worshippers, not only upon God's gift of grace, but also upon man's response, in the form of good works".[12] According to her great-niece Florence Austen, this was "a book of devotions always used by Jane Austen", suggesting that receiving "the Sacrament" (the name generally used for Holy Communion) was very important to her. On one occasion, in a letter to Cassandra, she records her "great pleasure" that two of her nephews, Edward and George Knight, young men whose heads seemed usually to be filled only with hunting and shooting, "were both at the Sacrament yesterday".[13]

In 1801 Second Lieutenant Charles Austen was given £30 prize money, with the expectation of £10 more to come, for his part in the capture of the French privateer *Le Scipio*. From this money he bought two gold chains, and two topaz crosses, amber in colour, for his sisters. Though she chided Charles for spending part of his prize money on a present for her, Jane was delighted with the gift: "... I shall write again by this post to thank and reproach him. – We shall be unbearably fine,"[14] she wrote to Cassandra. The sisters clearly treasured the crosses, as they were kept within the family and can be seen at Chawton Cottage to this day. Topaz was very fashionable at the time, and was used to make many different types of locket,[15] so Charles must have consciously decided to give his sisters a gift of a cross, a symbol of their Christian faith. Over ten years later, when she was writing *Mansfield Park*, Jane used this real-life incident in the story. William Price gives his sister the gift of an amber cross, which he has bought for her in Sicily, suggesting how significant Charles' gift was to her.

Three prayers, widely believed to have been written by Jane for use at Sunday-evening prayers at Chawton Cottage, have been found preserved in two manuscripts. The first manuscript, almost certainly in Cassandra's writing, on paper watermarked 1818, the year after Jane's death, is titled "Prayers composed by my ever dear sister Jane". The second manuscript gives no clue to a date, and is written in two hands, thought to be those of Jane and her brother Henry. The similarity of style in the prayers suggests that they are the composition of one writer, and the erratic grammar so closely matches the grammar of Jane's letters and the manuscripts of her novels that we can be confident that she wrote these prayers herself.

The prayers are given in full in the appendices to this book. In their tone and content they bear a resemblance to those of the litany of the Book of Common Prayer, with which Jane would have been very familiar. In these prayers we see a particular emphasis on the Fatherhood and the providence of God. The importance of self-examination and of the desire to respond to God's grace by a life well lived, both important themes in William Vickers' book, are also central themes:

Pardon oh! God the offences of the past day. We are conscious of many frailties; we remember with shame and contrition, many evil thoughts and neglected duties; and we have perhaps sinned against thee and against our fellow-creatures in many instances of which we have no remembrance. Pardon oh God! whatever thou hast seen amiss in us, and give us a stronger desire of resisting every evil inclination and weakening every habit of sin. (Prayer 2)

Another day is now gone, and added to those, for which we were before accountable. Teach us almighty father to consider this solemn truth, as we should do, that we may feel the importance of every day and every hour as it passes, and earnestly strive to make a better use of what thy goodness may yet bestow on us, than we have done of the time past. (Prayer 3)

A sentence in her first prayer shows us the reality of Jane Austen's faith to her:

Above all other blessings oh! God, for ourselves and our fellow-creatures, we implore thee to quicken our sense of thy mercy in the redemption of the world, of the value of that holy religion in which we have been brought up, that we may not, by our own neglect, throw away the salvation thou hast given us, nor be Christians only in name. (Prayer 1)

These last words, about not being Christian "only in name", suggest to us that Jane's Christian faith was not just a practice she had imbibed from her childhood, when she was daughter of the rectory, but that she had taken this faith as her own as a mature adult. Many followers of the Evangelical movement of her time, however, believed that they, the Evangelicals, were the only true Christians and that others were indeed Christians "only in name". Jane Austen makes several references to Evangelicals and Evangelicalism in her letters, and many critics believe that *Mansfield Park* was influenced by Evangelicalism. But what was it?

The Evangelical Movement

The term *evangelical* means "of the Gospel" and first became widely used in the eighteenth century as a description of the revival associated with John and Charles Wesley. This revival had roots in the religious, social, and ideological changes of earlier centuries, in particular the Reformation and its resulting pietistic movements in many parts of Europe. The hallmarks of the evangelical movement were repentance, spiritual rebirth, close relationships among believers, and practical care for the poor. The young Anglican clergyman John Wesley encountered such a group, of evangelical German Moravians, on a ship bound for America in 1735, and was intrigued by their faith. After his experience at Aldersgate on 24 May 1738, widely referred to as his conversion, when his heart was "strangely warmed", Wesley began a preaching and teaching ministry. He was joined by many others, clergy and lay people, whose public preaching, often out of doors, drew thousands. The converts from their preaching were grouped into "methodist societies" for further teaching and mutual support. Wesley and other leaders of the movement believed their doctrinal position to be entirely in accord with the teaching of the Church of England, but that they had rediscovered spiritual emphases that most other Anglicans appeared to ignore.

Evangelicals were noted for their fervour, which was described by their opponents as "enthusiasm". George Whitefield, another Evangelical Anglican clergyman, was repeatedly accused of "wild enthusiasm", and his preaching was seen as subversive and a provocation to riot. There was often an uneasy truce between the Evangelical leaders and the authorities of the Church of England, and in the later years of the nineteenth century many of the "methodist societies" of Evangelicals, which had been set up initially within Anglican parishes, now formed their own structure, as the Methodist Church, with their own authority outside the Church of England. However, some Evangelicals remained within it. One such, as we have seen, was Hannah More, and it was Jane Austen's dislike of Hannah More's didactic approach in her novel writing that led to the comment "I do not like the evangelicals". Yet just five years later we find her writing the opposite in a letter to her niece Fanny Knight. Fanny was seeking Jane's advice about a young man, John Plumptre, with whom she had previously fancied herself in love, but was now less sure about. Jane had already met John and liked him, and had found him "a very amiable young man, only too diffident to be as agreeable as he might be".[16] One of Fanny's concerns was that John wasn't as much fun as her brothers and was becoming more evangelical in his habits: "acting more strictly up to the precepts of the New Testament than others".[17] In her response to Fanny's dilemma, Jane first lists all the reasons in favour of Fanny continuing her relationship with John Plumptre, and it is the context of her praise of his character, "his uncommonly amiable mind, strict principles, just notions, good habits", that she writes: "I am by no means convinced that we ought not all to be evangelicals, and am at least persuaded that they who are so from reason and feeling, must be happiest and safest."[18] In a further letter to Fanny, Jane wrote: "I cannot suppose we differ in our ideas of the Christian religion. You have given an excellent description of it. We only affix a different meaning to the word *evangelical*."[19] Given the contradiction between Jane's comments, one speaking negatively and one positively about Evangelicalism, we must conclude that then, as now, people sometimes used the word "evangelical" to convey different things.

Most Anglican clergy of Jane Austen's day had studied first at Oxford or Cambridge University. Evangelicalism had a much stronger base at Cambridge, partly owing to the influence of the Evangelical rector of the town's Holy Trinity Church, Charles Simeon.[20] Most of Jane's family and clergy acquaintances were Oxford men and were largely untouched by the movement. An exception, however, as we have seen, was her cousin Edward Cooper, the rector of Hamstall Ridware in Staffordshire. Though he studied at All Souls College, Oxford, he became an ardent Evangelical.

We have already seen that Jane did not enjoy his company or the tone of his letters, and her dislike comes into sharp focus in her concern expressed to Cassandra following the death of their sister-in-law Elizabeth Knight in 1808: "I have written to Edward Cooper, and hope he will not send one of his letters of cruel comfort to my poor brother…"[21]

Edward Cooper had a number of books of sermons

published, and Jane's two recorded responses to these sermons give us clues about her response to his Evangelical theology: "Miss M. conveys to us a third volume of sermons, from Hamstall, just published, and which we are to like better than the two others; they are professedly *practical*, and for the use of country congregations,"[22] Jane wrote to Cassandra. This volume was entitled *Practical and Familiar Sermons, Designed for Parochial and Domestic Instruction* (1809). His earlier collections, to which Jane had responded much less favourably, were the 1803 collection *Examination of the Necessity of Sunday-Drilling* and his 1804 volume, which was described as "Sermons, chiefly designed to elucidate doctrines". In response to a later book of his sermons, which she received in 1816, Jane notes: "We do not much like Mr. Cooper's new sermons. They are fuller of regeneration and conversion than ever, with the addition of his zeal in the cause of the Bible Society."[23]

Jane did not view her cousin's doctrines with favour, and objected to his stress in this last book of sermons on the need for a dramatic conversion before faith could be evident, and the sense of superiority it suggests – that only those who had had an evangelical conversion experience were "proper Christians". She much preferred the collection of his sermons that were practical – sermons which related faith to the world around her. Indeed, in a letter to her niece Fanny Knight in 1817, Jane writes: "... you... have such excellent Judgement in what you do! – Religious Principle I fancy must explain it,"[24] suggesting that, for her, wise judgment about how one's life is led is the significant outworking of religion. So it is in the area of behaviour and morality that we must look first, to explore the outworking for Jane of her Christian spirituality during her Chawton years.

CHAPTER SIX

THE LATER NOVELS:
MANSFIELD PARK

Mansfield Park and Improvement

Jane Austen cared deeply about the welfare of her country. In a letter to her friend Martha Lloyd about the war with America[1] written in 1814, the year in which *Mansfield Park* was published, she wrote:

> *If we <u>are</u> to be ruined, it cannot be helped – but I place my hope of better things on a claim to the protection of Heaven, as a Religious Nation, a Nation inspite of much Evil improving in Religion.*[2]

The theme of improvement is introduced by name early on in the novel, when the Mansfield household go to visit Sotherton Court, the home of Maria's fiancé, Mr Rushworth. There is much talk of "improvements", for Sir Humphry Repton is soon to be invited in to "improve" the landscape of the Sotherton estate, so that it accords with the latest fashion of artificially created waterfalls, hillocks, and wide vistas. This will require the cutting down of the formal row of oaks that line the original approach to the house. Only Fanny of the party recognizes that what is really needed is the inner moral improvement of the occupants of Sotherton Court, rather than the outward improvement to its gardens and park.

As the novel progresses, different characters voice their understanding of what improving in religion means for them. For Mary Crawford, it means the ending of obligatory family prayers in the Sotherton Chapel, for "Every generation has its improvements," she claims. "Cannot you imagine with what unwilling feelings the former belles of the house of Rushworth did many a time repair to this chapel?" For Henry Crawford, it comes through increasing the social prestige of clergymen by the improvement of their rectories so that "from being the mere gentleman's residence, it becomes, by judicious improvement, the residence of a man of education, taste, modern manners, good connections". This shows how superficial his understanding of religion is. In a conversation following on from a reading aloud of Shakespeare, Edmund comments on changes in the delivery of church services, declaring that "[t]here is now a spirit of improvement abroad"; for, as compared to

> *"twenty, thirty, forty years ago… it is felt that distinctness and energy may have weight in recommending the most solid truths, and besides there is a more general observation and taste, a more critical knowledge diffused, than formerly; in every congregation there is a larger proportion who know a little of the matter, and who can judge and criticize."*

This leads Mr Crawford to conjecture on how he might like to preach:

> *"I never listened to a distinguished preacher in my life without a sort of envy. But then, I must have a London audience. I could not preach, but to the educated; to those who were capable of estimating my composition. And, I do not know that I should be fond of preaching often; now and then, perhaps, once or twice in the spring, after being anxiously expected for half a dozen*

*Sundays together; but not for a constancy; it would not do for a
constancy."*

This last comment causes Fanny involuntarily to shake her head,
aghast at the idea of Mr Crawford as a clergyman concerned
only with his eloquence, how he is heard, and with no concern
for faithfulness, for the inner commitment that she believes is so
essential in a clergyman. A clergyman's role, Jane is to suggest in
this novel, must primarily be to improve society.

Mansfield Park as a Microcosm of Jane's Society

In many ways, the emphasis on improvement in *Mansfield
Park* continues the tenor of her three earlier novels, *Sense and
Sensibility*, *Pride and Prejudice*, and *Northanger Abbey*, but there
are two new developments. Firstly, it is a much more overtly
religious book, reflecting a number of religious themes, and
containing a number of conversations between her characters
about the role of religion and the church in society. Secondly,
the scope of the novel is much broader than that of her first
three novels – with a concern not just for the improvement of
the individual characters in her story but for the improvement
of society.

In a letter to Francis written in July 1813, when she was
midway through writing the novel, Jane commented that she
was writing a book that was much more serious than *Pride and
Prejudice*, which was selling well at the time: "I have something in
hand – which I hope on the credit of P.&P. will sell well, tho' not
half so entertaining."[3]

Jane Austen rarely referred to national events in her novels,
but she was aware of events in the world outside the small village
of Chawton, as her reference to "the Nation" in her letter to
Martha Lloyd suggests. During the period from 1811 to 1813,

when she was writing *Mansfield Park*, the war with France was continuing, and there was social unrest in England. In addition, political matters at home were particularly turbulent. Madness had struck down the virtuous King George III, leading to the extravagant and licentious Prince of Wales becoming Regent and therefore head of state. Prime Minister Spencer Perceval had been murdered in the House of Commons. The riots initiated by the Luddites (textile workers from the Midlands and the north of England protesting against the new machines that would put them out of work) had been suppressed by a massive military force, further unsettling the status quo. Jane was aware that society was facing challenges.

The titles of Jane Austen's novels are always important. We know that because she often changed them as the novels developed. A title reflected the most important aspect of the story for her – maybe the main character, as in *Emma*, or the virtues and vices her characters have to engage with, as in *Sense and Sensibility* and *Pride and Prejudice*. *Northanger Abbey*, like *Emma*, was originally named after the leading character who has the greatest change to make in the novel – so Jane first called her story *Susan*, though she later changed it to *Catherine* after Susan was used by another novelist, as we have seen. When the novel was finally published posthumously, it had been renamed *Northanger Abbey* by her family. However, *Mansfield Park*, as far as we are aware, was never anything else in Jane Austen's mind. The dominant theme of the book, the title suggests, is not the heroine, Fanny Price, but the estate of Mansfield Park, which can be seen as a microcosm of the world of the English gentry that was Jane's social world. In her earlier novels, she had explored the ways in which her leading characters are affected by the challenges they face; in this one she considers how the future security of the estate of Mansfield Park is affected by the behaviour of her leading characters. It took her two and a half years to write, much the longest time of concentrated writing on any of her books. Given the wider scope of *Mansfield Park*, it is not surprising that its creation took so long.

In her earlier novels Jane Austen had been happy simply to mock those in high social positions – so John and Fanny Dashwood in *Sense and Sensibility* and Lady Catherine de Bourgh in *Pride and Prejudice* are critiqued within their social roles, but their right to their honoured place in society is not questioned. We have seen that a turning point in *Pride and Prejudice*, for many readers, is the moment when Elizabeth Bennet hears from the housekeeper of Pemberley what a good landlord Darcy's father had been and that "his son will be just like him – just as affable to the poor". Darcy is a good landlord who takes his responsibilities seriously, and all is therefore safe and well within the social structure of the world of *Pride and Prejudice*.

In *Mansfield Park*, however, we do not have the secure and happy picture of the housekeeper lauding the master of the house to the skies. We have Sir Thomas Bertram, the master of the house, going away to the West Indies, and many of his family not caring that he has gone away and even being greatly relieved by his absence. We have a dissolute elder son, Tom, frittering away the inheritance. We have the younger son, soon to be ordained, and the elder daughter being led astray morally by the wily Miss Crawford and the debonair Mr Crawford, recently come from London, a city that often represents vice in Jane Austen's novels. We have the destructive Mrs Norris, the lazy Lady Bertram, and the self-indulgent clergyman Dr Grant. In *Mansfield Park* Jane Austen portrays her own society being threatened, but the threats are internal and of its own making, and caused by neglect.

The Challenges Facing Mansfield Park

The society of Mansfield Park is being challenged from a number of different directions. Firstly, the poor parenting of Sir Thomas and Lady Bertram has resulted in all four of their children growing up unable to withstand temptation. There is concern about Tom's capability to run Mansfield Park financially and morally. His extravagance means that Sir Thomas can no longer afford to keep the Mansfield living open for Edmund after his ordination: "Tom's extravagance had… been so great as to render disposal of the next presentation necessary, and the younger brother must help to pay for the pleasures of the elder." Instead, Edmund is to serve at Thornton Lacey, eight miles distant, where Sir Thomas expects him to live. As he says of Edmund, "He knows that human nature needs more lessons than a weekly sermon can convey, and that if he does not live among his parishioners and prove himself by constant attention their well-wisher and friend, he does very little either for their good or his own."

After his ordination, however, even Edmund appears to be tempted to neglect his duties. Formerly the best-behaved son, he is to be found frequently at Mansfield, drawn by the attractions of Mary Crawford. Of the two sisters, Maria agrees to marry the unpromising Mr Rushworth in a fit of pique when she cannot secure the attentions of Henry Crawford. Mr Rushworth, though rich, is depicted as a pompous fool and it becomes evident later that Maria is unhappy and unfulfilled in her marriage. Julia shows herself to be as selfish and lacking in principles as her sister, as they compete for Crawford's attentions. Later, living with her sister, she too is tempted to behave badly.

It was not only upon Tom that the financial future of Mansfield depended, for its riches were built on the income generated by Sir Thomas' property in Antigua, in the West

Indies, which would have been a sugar plantation maintained by slave labour.[4] At the beginning of the novel there are problems with Sir Thomas' affairs in Antigua, requiring him to go out to his plantation, taking Tom with him. We are not told the nature of the problem, or whether or not it has been caused by difficulties in the supply of labour because of the ending of the transatlantic slave trade in 1807. Sir Thomas is able to sort the matter out, in the short term at least, so that the plantation is again able to yield the profits that are needed for Mansfield.

Like many families of her class at the time, Jane Austen's family had close connections with estate owners in the West Indies – two sisters-in-law came from such families, and her brother Charles served for some years on naval vessels in North America, protecting the West Indies from the French. For the inhabitants of Mansfield Park, Antigua is a source of wealth necessary for their comfortable life. This raises major problems for the discerning modern reader of the novel. A similar attitude, suggesting again that the worth of the colonies was viewed by many as being only what they could produce for the British market, is illustrated by Lady Bertram's impatience for William to go to India "that I may have a shawl. I think I will have two shawls."

After his return from Antigua, Fanny does question Sir Thomas about the slave trade, as is reported in a conversation between Fanny and Edmund the next day, though the precise nature of Fanny's question is unclear. Fanny is the first speaker: "... Did you hear me ask him about the slave trade last night?" Edmund replies: "I did and was in hopes the question would be followed up by others. It would have pleased your uncle to be inquired of further." Fanny then says: "And I longed to do it – but there was such a dead silence!"

The role of slavery in *Mansfield Park* is examined in depth in Edward W. Said's *Culture and Imperialism*. Said attributes "the dead silence" to the difficulty of such a discussion, "as one world could not be connected to the other since there is no common language for both",[5] though another possibility is that the silence was due to the boredom that the other young people felt with the topic. Said concludes that we have to recognize the different moral consciousness of different ages: "It would be silly to expect Jane Austen to treat slavery with anything like the passion of an abolitionist or a newly liberated slave."[6] We need to recognize that she was part of a slave-owning society. Thus although Jane Austen could not but be aware of the work of William Wilberforce[7] and his Evangelical colleagues in the repeal of the slave trade, Said argues that we do not know how she viewed such a reformation.

However, Paula Byrne suggests that we can clearly perceive Jane's anti-slavery stance in her choice of names in the novel.[8] Mansfield Park could be named after Lord Mansfield, who was on the side of abolition in the late eighteenth century. As Lord Chief Justice, he found against slave owners and slave traders in two widely reported cases,[9] his verdicts giving great encouragement to the abolitionist cause. By contrast, Mrs Norris, who treats Fanny so cruelly, shares her surname with Robert Norris, a slave trader in West Africa, who greatly damaged the abolitionists' cause with his claims that the slave trade had positive effects on Africa.

A further moral challenge to Mansfield Park comes from the Crawfords, outsiders who have just come from London, who have a different value system from that of the Mansfield rural community. So, in a throwaway comment about Mary Crawford, we learn that she comes from London where "everything is to be got by money". On another occasion Mary is unable to see, even after it has been explained to her, why she cannot get a man with a cart to transport her harp at harvest time. She does not understand that in the countryside social activities must at times give way to the demands of agriculture, which is the mainstay of rural life. We hear how infrequent are Mr Crawford's visits to his estate at Everingham – which leads the reader to question whether he can be a good landlord and master. An example of their undermining behaviour can be seen in Henry's determination to make Fanny fall in love with him – this is before he is consciously attracted to her – and Mary's collusion in this:

> *"It can be but for a fortnight," said Henry, "and if a fortnight can kill her, she must have a constitution which nothing could save. No! I will not do her any harm, dear little soul! I only want her to look kindly on me, to give me smiles as well as blushes… to think as I think, be interested in all my possessions and pleasures, try to keep me longer at Mansfield, and feel when I go away that she shall never be happy again. I want nothing more."*
> *"Moderation itself!" said Mary… And without attempting any further remonstrance, she left Fanny to her fate…*

Finally, the society of Mansfield Park is threatened by another internal force: Dr Grant, the Mansfield clergyman, has such a dilatory sense of his duty that he is unable to be a moral influence. As with the clerical Mr Collins of *Pride and Prejudice*, there is humour in Jane Austen's portrayal of the indolent and indulgent Dr Grant in his social role, as is reflected in this description of him by his sister-in-law, Mary Crawford:

> *"… though Dr Grant is most kind and obliging to me, and though he is really a gentleman, and I dare say a good scholar and clever, and often preaches good sermons, and is very respectable, I see him to be an indolent, selfish bon vivant, who must have his palate consulted in every thing, who will not stir a finger for the convenience of any one, and who, moreover, if the cook makes a blunder, is out of humour with his excellent wife. To own the*

*truth, Henry and I were partly driven out this very evening, by
a disappointment about a green goose, which he could not get the
better of. My poor sister was forced to stay and bear it."*

The first words used of Dr Grant are that he is "a hearty man
of forty five... a short-necked apoplectic sort of fellow" who,
"plied well with good things, would soon pop off". We first
encounter him directly when he is complaining about the poor
quality of the apricots in his garden. Dr Grant's appearances
in the novel are almost entirely in scenes where he is eating
and drinking, so we can conclude that he is more concerned
with enjoying the material benefits of his role as the Mansfield
clergyman than he is with carrying out his spiritual duties.

Symbolism in the Novel

As we have noted, the wilderness at Sotherton was a
fashionable feature, a contrast to the more formal gardens
nearer the house where everything was controlled. It is in the
wilderness of Sotherton that Edmund begins to succumb to
the temptations of Mary Crawford, leaving Fanny alone. At
the edge of the wilderness are the locked park gates – and
it is Maria who first voices a longing to go through them to
the open world beyond. Mr Rushworth goes to get the key,
and she says to Crawford: "... that iron gate, that ha-ha, give
me a feeling of restraint and hardship. 'I cannot get out,'
as the starling said." Henry Crawford encourages Maria to
pass through without the key, for with his help they can both
squeeze through a gap:

*"I think you might with little difficulty pass round the edge of
the gate, here, with my assistance; I think it might be done, if
you really wished to be more at large, and could allow yourself to
think it not prohibited."*

When Mr Rushworth returns with the key, it is to find Maria has escaped past the gate with Mr Crawford, and they are gone – a symbolic prefiguring of their elopement later in the story.

The play *Lovers' Vows* also has a strong role in the novel. Only Fanny recognizes that the leading female roles of Agatha (to be played by Maria) and Amelia (by Mary Crawford) are quite improper – "the situation of one, and the language of the other, so unfit to be expressed by any woman of modesty". Fanny's concern that acting such a part can give rise to an erosion of moral restraints is justified, as the acting does influence the real lives of the actors. All the cast begin to behave more selfishly as they get absorbed in their roles and as Tom's plans for the play become more extravagant and unrealistic. Edmund overcomes his earlier moral opposition to the play because acting the part of Anhalt gives him the opportunity to play opposite Mary Crawford, and their love scenes lead him to become more infatuated by her. As for Maria and Henry Crawford, Fanny observes that Henry acted well, but "Maria she also thought acted well – too well", suggesting that Fanny could see that Maria was possibly not needing to act at all; that, despite being engaged to Mr Rushworth, she was actually falling in love with Henry Crawford. Jane Austen shows how Maria's repeated minor crossings of moral boundaries before her marriage set the scene for the major moral transgression later on.

The Importance of the Role of Fanny Price

Another significant difference between *Mansfield Park* and Jane Austen's other novels is in the role of her heroine, Fanny Price. In *Mansfield Park*, the whole community needs improvement, except for Fanny herself – she hardly needs to change at all. Uniquely in *Mansfield Park*, in the final chapter, Jane Austen refers to her as "My Fanny", which suggests her strong approbation of Fanny's character. Unlike her other heroines, Fanny escapes criticism from her creator. Once she has overcome her timidity, which has been understandably caused by the abrupt move, when she was only nine, from her small Portsmouth home to the large mansion at Mansfield, her task is only to develop and mature, for she is primarily to stay true to who she is, because all her virtues are already in place. "She is never, ever, wrong," claims the critic Tony Tanner. "Jane Austen, usually so ironic about her heroines, in this instance vindicates Fanny Price without qualification."[10] As Edmund says, "Fanny is the only one who has judged rightly throughout; who has been consistent." The whole spiritual responsibility for Mansfield Park falls on Fanny. Tony Tanner suggests that Fanny Price *saves* Mansfield Park. That is very religious language, but I would suggest that *Mansfield Park* is a very religious book.

While it is Tom's illness and subsequent change of behaviour that leads to Mansfield being saved materially, it is Fanny's constancy and other aspects of her character that inspire Sir Thomas to change his values, which saves Mansfield morally and spiritually. Thus Fanny's "saving of Mansfield Park" is not primarily through anything that she does, but through her virtues: through the morals she holds internally, and the manners she exhibits to the outside world. As Tony Tanner continues:

> ... at its most profound, it is a book about the difficulty of preserving true moral consciousness amid the selfish manoeuvring and jostling of society... Jane Austen knew that virtue was a hard affair and morality might involve renunciation, sacrifice and solitary anguish... In the debilitated but undeviating figure of Fanny Price we should perceive the pain and labour involved in maintaining true values in a corrosive world of dangerous energies and selfish power-play. She suffers in her stillness. For Righteousness' sake.[11]

Constancy is Fanny's most important virtue. Through the novel her other virtues are revealed, including humility, stillness, compassion, moral courage, and integrity. It is important also to note that Fanny's lack of charm is crucial to Jane Austen's intentions. In contrast, the Crawfords are frequently described in terms of their charm. "Charm", Alasdair MacIntyre suggests, "is the characteristically modern quality which those who lack or simulate the virtues use to get by in the situations of characteristically modern social life... Fanny is charmless, she has only the virtues..."[12]

As the novel progresses, Fanny stands more and more alone as only she sees where things are wrong, and she refuses to be compromised. In this respect Fanny plays the role of a prophet – sometimes also called a "seer" – of the Old Testament, whose stories Jane would have known from her childhood. The earlier challenges that Fanny faces, in the teasing of Maria and Julia, the harshness of Mrs Norris in her childhood, and the later apparent loss of Edmund to Mary Crawford, the pressure to take a part in the Mansfield theatricals: all these enable her to develop the habits of overcoming disappointment, of withstanding inner pain, of maintaining her commitment to doing what she knows to be right. Thus she has the inner strength to stand firm for what is right, when she faces the biggest test of all. She is able to withstand the deceiving charm of both Mary and Henry Crawford, and to hold steadfast against the pressure from Sir Thomas and Edmund to marry Mr Crawford. She holds out alone even in exile in Portsmouth, when marrying Henry Crawford becomes a more attractive prospect, in contrast to the squalor of her surroundings and the drawbacks of the society she is condemned to share. Tom's illness brings the Bertram crisis to a head, and Fanny's worth is finally recognized and she is called home to Mansfield. When Crawford finally elopes with Maria, his true nature is at last exposed, and everyone else finally sees this. Edmund at last recognizes Mary Crawford's moral deficiencies when she makes it clear that it is the discovery of her brother's adultery that she regrets, not the act itself. Married to Fanny, Edmund can now be the dedicated clergyman he felt himself called to be before he was led astray by Mary Crawford.

We have asserted that Fanny *saves* Mansfield Park through her virtues – in what sense can it be said that Mansfield Park is *saved*? At the end of the novel the future of Mansfield is secured: it is secured religiously, because Edmund, a resident clergyman with his strong sense of vocation and duty restored, has come to the Mansfield living; it is secured financially, because Sir Thomas' financial affairs are now in order and Tom, the elder son, has reformed and accepted his responsibilities; and it is secured morally because we can now be confident in the sense of responsibility of the next generation who will lead Mansfield Park after Sir Thomas dies. Sir Thomas has recognized Fanny's virtues, the virtues he will now seek to emulate as he takes Mansfield Park into the future. Fanny, who once was ignored, sidelined, and then sent into exile back in Portsmouth, has been vindicated and welcomed back as a daughter of the house.

In the last chapter of *Mansfield Park*, we have a judgment scene, where Jane Austen pronounces, albeit reluctantly, the future destinies of all the characters: "Let other pens dwell on guilt and misery. I quit such odious subjects as soon as I can, impatient to restore everybody, not greatly in fault themselves, to tolerable comfort, and to have done with all the rest." Tom, Edmund, and Julia have been restored to their rightful places in the family – for Tom "had suffered and he had learned to think, two advantages that he had never known before"; Edmund has ended his relationship with Mary Crawford and recognized that it is Fanny who should be his wife; and Julia was "humble and wishing to be forgiven…" Others, though, are sent away from Mansfield, and Jane Austen suggests that they give themselves their own punishment. In Portsmouth, Fanny had reminded Crawford about his conscience: "We have all a better guide in ourselves, if we would attend to it, than any other person can be." Now we learn that Henry was aware of his conscience before the affair with Maria, but that he was not strong enough to follow it: "Had he done as he intended, and as he knew he ought, by going down to Everingham after his return from Portsmouth, he might have been deciding his own happy destiny… for his mind was unused to make any sacrifice to right…" Henry suffers the public punishment of disgrace: "… without presuming to look forward to a juster hereafter, we may fairly consider a man of sense like Henry Crawford to be providing for himself no small portion of vexation and regret…" Henry now recognizes, too late, all he has lost in losing Fanny. Mrs Norris and Maria are "shut up together with little society, on one side no affection, on the other, no judgement, it may be reasonably supposed that their tempers became their mutual punishment". Dr Grant is banished from village life – first Jane Austen sends him to Bath for a few months, and then he is sent permanently to London, where he has secured a stall at Westminster Abbey.[13] Given Jane Austen's personal dislike of the society in Bath, and the antipathy expressed in the novel to the ostentation of church life in London, she has chosen her places of exile for Dr Grant with care. His greed brings about his premature death; soon after arriving in London, he dies of apoplexy caused "by three great institutionary dinners in one week".

But who is Fanny, this saviour of Mansfield? And her brother William – the only person in Fanny's life who has constantly supported and believed in her – who is he? They are the poor relations. Together, Fanny and William are the antithesis of the sort of people whom Jane Austen, with her genteel and Tory upbringing, might have expected to be persons of influence. In *Mansfield Park*, where those whose duty it was to lead and to teach have let their community down, others more morally fitted, even if they are from a different social class, can, and should, take their place.

The final mark of salvation in the novel is that the influence of Mansfield has permeated beyond the walls of the Park to Fanny's brothers and sisters, for her sister Susan comes to Mansfield, with the expectation that her character will soon be reformed there, and there is a promise of help for more of the Price siblings.

The person whom Fanny has influenced the most, however, is Sir Thomas. At the close of the book he reflects on the difference between Fanny and his daughters:

> *Something must have been wanting **within** … He feared that principle, active principle, had been wanting, that they had never been properly taught to govern their inclinations and tempers, by that sense of duty which can alone suffice. They had been instructed theoretically in their religion, but never required to bring it into daily practice… he had meant them to be good, but his cares had been directed to the understanding and manners, not to the disposition; and of the necessity of self-denial and humility, he feared they had never heard from any lips that could profit them.*

Sir Thomas realizes that, for all their expensive education, his daughters had not developed the habits of virtue that Fanny had learned through her hard childhood. When Maria and Julia were tempted and tested, they had no substantial character formation to rely on, to help them to behave appropriately:

> *Bitterly did he deplore a deficiency which now he could scarcely comprehend to have been possible. Wretchedly did he feel, that with all the cost and care of an anxious and expensive*

education, he had brought up his daughters, without their
understanding their first duties, or his being acquainted with their
character and temper.

So Mansfield Park is reinvigorated with a renewed baronet restored to his sense of duty, and a competent and committed clergyman living next door. The Crawfords, with all their deceiving charm, have gone. We can look to the future of Mansfield Park with confident assurance. This is Jane Austen's vision of how society should be.

The Role of the Church and the Clergy

As we have seen, Jane Austen makes it clear that a major factor in the threat to the future of Mansfield Park is the dilatoriness of Dr Grant, the clergyman of Mansfield. Despite his own moral weaknesses, Edmund Bertram speaks very forcefully about the potential role and influence of the church and the clergy, if clergy took their duties as seriously as they ought. As Fanny Price is heard to agree with all his hopes, Edmund's words may well reveal Austen's own thinking. At Sotherton Court, we learn of Edmund's support for the practice of regular family prayers. Later conversations in the novel reveal his and his father's view that clergy should always live within the parish they serve, not just to ensure their ready availability for Sunday services but because they have a role all through the week in being a moral influence for the good of the society around them. Edmund sees the role of clergy as being to preach, to teach, and to lead the community by their example. He stresses the importance of preaching sermons that are accessible to the congregation, and of the regular provision of the Sacrament.

All that Jane Austen put into the mouths of Edmund Bertram and Fanny Price of *Mansfield Park* about the reform that was needed in the practice of the clergy, and therefore the need to rediscover the clerical profession as a vocation and not just a livelihood, very much reflects one aspect of the aspirations of the Evangelicals[14] of her time. Mary Crawford might believe that "a clergyman has nothing to do but to be slovenly and selfish – read the newspaper, watch the weather, and quarrel with his wife. His curate does all the work, and the business of his own life is to dine", but attitudes were now changing in many parts of the church, and not just in its evangelical wing. Jane's godfather, Revd Samuel Cooke, concurred with her, for, in a collection of comments about *Mansfield Park*, she notes:

> *Mr & Mrs Cooke – very much pleased with it – particularly with the Manner in which the Clergy are treated. – Mr Cooke called it "the most sensible Novel he had ever read."*[15]

In the novel, Edmund comments: "... as the clergy are, or are not, what they ought to be, so are the rest of the nation". It was in the changing attitude and approach of the clergy, with their consequent benefits for society, that Jane perceived her nation was "improving in religion" at the time that *Mansfield Park* was published.

CHAPTER SEVEN

THE LATER NOVELS:
EMMA AND *PERSUASION*

Emma

Jane Austen's penultimate completed novel was *Emma*, which was published in 1814. In it, the action is set in the community of Highbury, and here Jane Austen moves back from the country-estate setting of Mansfield Park to her more usual village setting, thereby returning to the familiar pattern of a novel based on the lives of "three or four families in a neighbourhood", charting their social interaction, through visits, balls, and outings. But there is a significant difference from her earlier novels for, until *Emma*, most of her heroes and heroines, before they can be united, have had to overcome some great external obstacle – their difference in social class, family objections, or lack of money. There is nothing external that prevents Emma and Mr Knightley from recognizing the possibility of their love and marriage at the beginning of the book; the obstacles are all within Emma. Her overactive imagination, her self-delusion, and her desire to manipulate others for her own amusement and control are the barriers that need to be overcome before she can be rewarded with such happiness. "I am going to take a heroine whom no one but myself will much like,"[1] Jane Austen told her family, and so she began the story of Emma, setting the scene in the book's opening sentence: "Emma Woodhouse, handsome, clever, and rich, with a comfortable home and happy disposition, seemed to unite some of the best blessings of existence; and had lived nearly twenty-one years in the world with very little to distress or vex her." Emma has not yet suffered, Jane Austen tells us at the outset of the book, suggesting that Emma has therefore not learned anything useful in her life thus far.

Emma has the attraction of a good mind, but after the marriage of her governess she is left at home with only her aging father for company. She has too little to occupy her time and her mind – though in this, as in so much else, she is self-deluded, for she declares: "Mine is an active, busy mind with a great many independent resources." Having, as she believes, successfully brought about one marriage through her matchmaking, she is keen to repeat that achievement, and so she begins to meddle in the lives of other people.

It is harder for the reader to grasp the events in the story and the intentions of the main characters in *Emma* than in Jane Austen's other novels. This is because Jane Austen employs the free indirect writing style, now well used by contemporary writers. It is thought by some literary critics to have been first used in *Emma*, and therefore created by Jane Austen herself.[2] Although the narration is in the third person, the narrator's voice is usually imbued with that of Emma; thus the story is told through Emma's consciousness, and her understanding of events and of herself is often partial, mistaken, and self-deluding. For most of the novel, then, through this deception on the part of the authorial voice, the reader's perception of events and of Emma's character is as flawed as Emma's own self-understanding. Since Emma believes that Mr Elton is in love with Harriet, and Mr Churchill with herself, the reader tends to believe this too. Emma has no perception that she and Mr Knightley are so well matched, so the reader is as surprised as Emma when she finally realizes that "Mr Knightley must marry no-one but herself".

When we consider *Emma* through the lens of spirituality, we see the greatness of the challenge that Jane Austen set herself, for she has a harder and longer task than she had with her earlier heroines to bring this self-satisfied heroine to the point of self-reflection, where she can acknowledge and learn from her mistakes. She needs to begin to develop patience and understanding, realize that she must stop meddling in other peoples' lives, and display the Christian virtue of charity in her attitudes as well as in her actions.

As with all of Jane Austen's heroines, it is through the experience of loss, when she thinks she has lost Mr Knightley to Harriet, that Emma is brought up short and makes such a resolution:

> *the only source whence anything like composure could be drawn, was in the resolution of her own better conduct, and the hope that, however inferior in spirit and gaiety might be the following and every winter of her life to the past, it would yet find her more rational, more acquainted with herself, and leave her less to regret when it were gone.*

This is the only one of Jane Austen's novels in which there is more than a passing reference to the wedding of the heroine and hero. However, her purpose in saying more about Emma and Mr Knightley's wedding is not to describe the superficial elegance or festivities, but to point out the importance of the celebration to those who have the ability to reflect on the deep inner meaning of the marriage, rather than on any outward show of wedding finery:

> *The wedding was very much like other weddings, where the parties have no taste for finery or parade; and Mrs Elton, from*

the particulars detailed by her husband, thought it all extremely shabby, and very inferior to her own. "Very little white satin, very few lace veils; a most pitiful business! Selina would stare when she heard of it." But, in spite of these deficiencies, the wishes, the hopes, the confidence, the predictions of the small band of true friends who witnessed the ceremony, were fully answered in the perfect happiness of the union.

Emma is also the only novel of Jane Austen's in which we encounter a clergyman in his religious duties – for we meet Mr Elton embarking on a visit to the poor. He is commended for his conscientious visiting of some of his poorer parishioners, as we have seen – but this seems to be his only commendation. Otherwise, he comes across as self-seeking in his desire to marry Emma so that he can gain her fortune, and shallow in his very quick subsequent marriage to Augusta Hawkins. Clearly his attachment to Emma was illusory, given how quickly he finds someone else. He is also uncharitable in his treatment of Harriet by refusing to dance with her at the ball, and weak-willed as he becomes more and more dominated by his new wife. With Mr Elton unable or unwilling to provide a moral lead, it is usually left to Mr Knightley to do so. It is he, not Mr Elton, although he is one of the party, who remonstrates with Emma after her rudeness to Miss Bates at Box Hill:

I cannot see you acting wrong, without a remonstrance. How could you be so unfeeling to Miss Bates? How could you be so insolent in your wit to a woman of her character, age, and situation? Emma, I had not thought it possible.

Unlike the more remote settings of the villages in her first four novels, Highbury is just sixteen miles from London, near enough for Frank Churchill to visit for a day. Emma (and thus the reader also) understands that he travels all the way to London for the sole purpose of having a haircut – an excursion which provides Emma with her first doubt about the steadfastness of his character, though she soon is able to conjure a reason to excuse him. The nearness of the urban is felt strongly in *Emma*, with a corresponding awareness of living in changing social times. So there is a wider social mix of people within the Highbury neighbourhood than we have seen in Jane Austen's previous novels, with people like Mr Perry, the apothecary, and Mrs Goddard, who runs a boarding school in Highbury, playing an active part. However, though often present at social events, their lower social status is still observed by their arriving after the dinner that has been enjoyed by their social superiors. Emma is particularly class-conscious and faces a dilemma over whether she can accept a dinner invitation from the Coles, who have made their money in trade and are thus her social inferiors:

> *The Coles were very respectable in their way, but they ought to be taught that it was not for them to arrange the terms on which the superior families would visit them. This lesson, she very much feared, they would receive only from herself; she had little hope of Mr Knightley, none of Mr Weston.*

Emma decides that she will go to the Coles' dinner party – not from any developing ethical principle, but because Frank Churchill will be there: her own self-centred reason for wanting to be present. Through the attitudes of Mr Knightley and Mr Weston, however, Jane is perhaps commending a greater social mixing, in certain circumstances, between the gentry and the professional and middle classes.

Emma has already taken on the socially inferior Harriet as her protégée, but she can justify this because, in her imagination, she has decided that Harriet's parents *may* have been people of importance. Her taking up of Harriet brings Emma into sharp dispute with Mr Knightley, however, who believes that Emma's appropriation of Harriet will make Emma more conceited and give Harriet the wrong perception of her place in society, leading her to feel dissatisfied with people from her own class. Mr Knightley's fears are proved true as, under Emma's guidance, Harriet rejects a marriage proposal from the yeoman farmer Robert Martin – and so manipulative is Emma that Harriet thinks that she has rejected Mr Martin of her own accord. Harriet now goes on to imagine herself loved by men of a higher social class, first by Mr Elton, and then by Mr Knightley. Finally, however, after Emma's repentance and reformation, Harriet gratefully accepts Mr Martin's renewed proposal.

A telling gauge of Emma's moral development through the novel is her changing attitude to the socially lower Martin family. Initially she is crudely snobbish, telling Harriet: "The yeomanry are precisely the order of people with whom I feel I can have nothing to do." Later we see a tension within Emma between her conscience and her prejudice:

> *She would have given a good deal, endured a good deal, to have had the Martins in a higher rank of life. They were so deserving, that a **little** higher could have been enough: but as it was, how could she have done otherwise? – Impossible! – She could not repent. They must be separated, but there was a great deal of pain in the process…*

With her reformation at the end of the novel, when she hears that Harriet and Mr Martin's engagement has finally been settled, we learn that for Emma now "it would be a great pleasure to know Robert Martin". The yeoman farmer marked a new type for Jane Austen to include as one of her cast of characters.

Following on from *Mansfield Park*, in *Emma* we see Jane Austen continuing to demonstrate a widening social perspective, recognizing the moral integrity and place in society of characters who are not "of the gentry". Knowing the story of Jane Austen's own "wilderness years" makes some of the characters in *Emma* seem particularly poignant and significant. Jane Fairfax is without an income and is forced to seek employment as a governess, for being a governess or a teacher was the only occupation open to an educated woman who had to make her own living. She is heard to liken being a governess to being in slavery. If that truly was Jane Austen's own opinion, then perhaps the comment of Miss Watson in the earlier *The Watsons* is also from Jane Austen's heart: "I would rather do anything than be a teacher in a school."[3] Perhaps she wondered how close she had come, a few years earlier, to having to offer herself as a governess or a teacher. There is great pathos too in her depiction of Mrs Bates and her garrulous spinster daughter, Miss Bates, who are so dependent on the charity of the people of Highbury. For Mrs Bates, like Mrs Austen, was an impecunious clergy widow. Without the generous gift of their home, Chawton Cottage, from Edward, and their household income from her other brothers, Mrs Austen could have been a Mrs Bates, and Jane could herself have been a Miss Bates. After her put-down of Miss Bates at the Box Hill picnic, Emma's repentance is a turning point in the novel – and there are great parallels between Emma's contrition and these words of one of Jane Austen's prayers:

> *Incline us Oh God! to think humbly of ourselves, to be severe only in the examination of our own conduct, to consider our fellow-creatures with kindness, and to judge all they say and do with that charity which we would desire from them themselves.*

The Dedication of *Emma*

Emma is dedicated to "His Royal Highness, the Prince Regent" – a most unexpected dedication, given Jane Austen's anonymity as a writer and her chosen provincial life. It was Dr Baillie, who treated Jane's brother Henry, and who was also one of the Prince Regent's physicians, who revealed to the Prince the identity of Jane Austen as the anonymous "author of Pride and Prejudice etc". As the Prince was a great admirer of these novels, he instructed his librarian and domestic chaplain, Revd James Stanier Clarke, to invite the authoress to visit Carlton House so that he could suggest that she dedicate her next book to him. Jane duly went to visit Carlton House, though its opulence failed to encourage her to raise her low opinion of the Prince Regent's extravagances. She politely declined the invitation to dedicate her next book, *Emma*, to him. Subsequent conversations with family and friends, however, led her to realize that the invitation was in fact a royal command, rather than a suggestion, and so the dedication in *Emma* was hastily arranged. In a subsequent letter, Mr Stanier Clarke, of his own volition this time, suggested that she might base her next novel on a very different type of clergyman from the provincial Mr Collins and Mr Elton – a clergyman, Mr Clarke suggested, who divided his time between the metropolis and the county, devoting his time to literature but remaining affectionate and demure:

> ... *much novelty may be introduced – shew dear Madam what good would be done if Tythes were taken away entirely, and describe him burying his own mother – as I did ... Carry your clergyman to Sea as the Friend of some distinguished Naval Character about the Court...* [4]

Her reply to Mr Clarke was polite but firm:

> *You are very kind in your hints as to the sort of composition which*
> *might recommend me at present, and I am fully sensible that an*
> *historical romance, founded on the House of Saxe-Cobourg, might*
> *be much more to the purpose of profit or popularity than such*
> *pictures of domestic life in country villages as I deal in. But I*
> *could no more write a romance than an epic poem. I could not sit*
> *seriously down to write a serious romance under any other motive*
> *than to save my life; and if it were indispensable for me to keep*
> *it up and never relax into laughing at myself or at other people,*
> *I am sure I should be hung before I had finished the first chapter.*
> *No, I must keep to my own style and go on in my own way; and*
> *though I may never succeed again in that, I am convinced that I*
> *should totally fail in any other.*[5]

Having politely declined to pursue Clarke's idea, and for the amusement of her family, she produced a "Plan of a Novel, according to hints from various quarters", as a spoof on the suggestion of the pompous Mr Clarke. The plot concerns a clergyman, who is an "Enthusiast in Literature" and "most zealous in his discharge of Pastoral Duties", and his most accomplished daughter, who converse together in long speeches, elegant language, and a tone of high serious sentiment. The daughter is told of her father's adventures before he married her mother, which included his going to sea as Chaplain to a Distinguished Naval Character, burying his mother, and giving his opinion on tithes. As the story continues the heroine and her father are never more than a fortnight in the same place, for they are driven all over Europe by a heartless young man who is pursuing the daughter with unrelenting passion. A host of other characters appear who are either exceptionally good or depravedly wicked, and the daughter is continually needing to be rescued by her father or some other hero. Finally, they are compelled to flee to Kamchatka, where the father expires "in a fine burst of Literary Enthusiasm, intermingled with Invectives against Holders of Tythes".[6]

Jane Austen had lost none of the fertile imagination or satirical wit that created the *Juvenilia* of her teenage years, but she would not be pressed to write for the public of a world outside her own experience.

Jane Austen might not feel equipped to write a "serious romance", as envisaged by Mr Stanier Clarke, but, four months before the publication of *Emma* in December 1815, she began work on her sixth full-length novel, a romance centred on the most experienced of all her heroines, the serious Anne Elliot of *Persuasion*.

Persuasion

Jane Austen may have developed the idea for her next novel from some correspondence that she had with her niece Fanny Knight at the end of 1814, just a few weeks before she began to write *Persuasion*. Fanny was contemplating embarking on an engagement that was likely to last for six or seven years, and she asked her Aunt Jane for her advice. Jane expressed the view that she could see her niece finding happiness in marriage to her suitor but not in a long engagement:

> *I should dread the continuance of this sort of tacit engagement, with such an uncertainty as there is of **when** it may be completed. Years may pass before he is independent; you like him well enough to marry but not well enough to wait...*[7]

Jane's reasoning is that Fanny is still young and has met few young men, and Jane is not convinced that her niece has truly found a deep, lasting love. She fears that Fanny may still meet someone whom she loves more, but then feel honour-bound to her first engagement (as happened to Edward in his loveless betrothal to Lucy Steele in *Sense and Sensibility*). In the same letter, however, Jane backs away from the position that she feels Fanny has put her in, as a "persuader": "But indeed you must not let anything depend on my opinion," she continues to Fanny; "your own feelings, and none but your own, should determine such an important point."[8]

Seven years before the story of *Persuasion* opens, the motherless Anne Elliot had allowed herself to be persuaded against marrying Captain Frederick Wentworth by Lady Russell, her godmother and once her mother's closest friend. Fear of a long, indefinite engagement before Wentworth could be in a financial position to marry Anne was one of the reasons for Lady Russell's advice. Since then, neither Anne nor Wentworth have found new love elsewhere. When the novel opens, Captain Wentworth is home from the sea with enough prize money to be in a position to marry, but when his and Anne's paths finally cross again, he is determined to marry someone, anyone, else. She has to suffer the pain of seeing him often, of loving him in the same way, as he casts his eye over other women and appears to be wooing one in particular. It is only after a few months of being together in the same group of people that Wentworth finally has to acknowledge to himself that he still loves Anne Elliot. In the meantime, she also has to fend off a new suitor, her cousin William Elliot.

Jane Austen left the novel untitled – the title *Persuasion* was chosen by her brother Henry when the book was published posthumously,[9] to reflect the theme that runs throughout the novel. Persuasion involves gaining power or influence over another person so that they take on your opinion, so it can be morally positive or negative, depending on the outcome and the motivation of the person doing the persuading. The nature of persuasion is explored in different ways in the novel, including many instances of self-persuasion leading to self-delusion – in particular, Anne's father, Sir Walter, and sisters Elizabeth and Mary are deluded, while Anne, by contrast, faces facts with bravery and quiet reflection. After being on the receiving end of persuasion, Anne now finds herself being given the role of persuader at Uppercross, where she is staying with Mary and her husband, Charles Musgrove.

> *"I wish you could persuade Mary not to be always fancying herself ill" was Charles' language; and, in an unhappy mood, thus spoke Mary: "I do believe if Charles were to see me dying, he would not think there was anything the matter with me. I am sure, Anne, if you would, you might persuade him that I really am very ill – a great deal worse than I ever own."*

What initially draws Wentworth to Louisa Musgrove is that, in complete contrast to Anne, she asserts that she will always follow her own path: "No – I have no idea of being so easily persuaded," she proclaims over one issue. But it is this attitude that leads to the reckless obstinacy that causes her accident on the Cobb, when she insists on jumping down from too great a height before anyone is ready to catch her. Reflecting on the accident:

> *Anne wondered whether it ever occurred to him now, to question the justness of his own previous opinion as to the universal felicity and advantage of firmness of character; and whether it might not strike him that, like all other qualities of the mind, it should have its proportions and limits. She thought it could scarcely escape him to feel that a persuadable temper might sometimes be as much in favour of happiness as a very resolute character.*

Right judgment is needed to discern whether it is right or wrong to seek to persuade others, or to heed the persuasion of others, within the particular circumstances of the situation. Anne's conclusion about Lady Russell's persuasion seven years before is that Lady Russell was in error for giving such advice, but that she had been right in submitting to it, for Lady Russell had been in the place of a parent to her. So, Anne concludes, "… if I had done otherwise, I should have suffered more in continuing the engagement than I did even in giving it up, because I should have suffered in my conscience."

It is a refreshing change in *Persuasion* to find a clergyman who is conscientious and diligent in the care of his parish – but ironically Dr Shirley does not appear in person and is the cause of strong criticism by Henrietta Musgrove, for she wants him to retire to the seaside, enabling her cousin, Revd Charles Hayter, to take his place, which would put him in a position to marry her. "I think it quite melancholy to have such excellent people as Dr and Mrs Shirley, who have been doing good all their lives, wearing out their last days in a place like Uppercross," Henrietta complains. "My only doubt is, whether anything could persuade him to leave his parish. He is so very strict and scrupulous in his notions; over-scrupulous I must say."

Unlike Mary Bennet of *Pride and Prejudice*, whose study had not given her any wisdom, Anne Elliot has practical advice to offer. When visiting the recently bereaved Captain Benwick in Lyme, Anne finds that his passion for poetry has led him to large doses of verse, which has given him no help in struggling against his sorrow:

> … *she ventured to recommend a larger allowance of prose in his daily study; and on being requested to particularise, mentioned such works of our best moralists, such collections of the finest letters, such memoirs of characters of worth and suffering, as*

occurred to her at the moment as calculated to rouse and fortify the mind by the highest precepts, and the strongest examples of moral and religious endurances.

Jane Austen reminds us that, as happened to Marianne Dashwood of *Sense and Sensibility*, reflection of the wrong sort will lead Captain Benwick into wallowing self-indulgence and self-pity. The works that Anne hopes to persuade him to read will help him to cope better with his loss.

A strong similarity with Jane's previous novel *Mansfield Park* is the winning virtue of constancy. Anne may have heeded Lady Russell's advice seven years earlier to give up the engagement, but she has not stopped loving. In a conversation with Captain Harville about constancy, Anne concludes: "All the privilege I claim for my own sex... is that of loving longest, when existence or when hope is gone!" These words are overheard by Captain Wentworth, and his immediate response is to write a declaration of love to Anne, explaining that, despite his apparent dalliance with Louisa, he too has remained constant, though he has had to let go of his anger and forgive her for the hurt she has caused him:

Dare not say that man forgets sooner than woman, that his love has an earlier death. I have loved none but you. Unjust I may have been, weak and resentful I have been, but never inconstant.

The last chapter of *Mansfield Park* explores the biblical theme of judgment. In the penultimate chapter of *Persuasion* Jane Austen again uses biblical language, this time to describe the reward given to Anne and Captain Wentworth for their constancy. For, in relating their reunion in the "quiet and retired gravel-walk", she writes: "... where the power of conversation would make the present hour a blessing indeed; and prepare it for all the immortality which the happiest recollections of their own future lives could bestow." By using the language of blessing and immortality, Jane Austen is suggesting that Anne and Captain Wentworth have acted righteously in a religious sense, and are thus being rewarded by God.

A very different destiny, however, is rolled out for Sir Walter Elliot, Anne's father. It is with Sir Walter that the novel begins:

> *Sir Walter Elliot, of Kellynch Hall, in Somersetshire, was a man who, for his own amusement, never took up any book but the Baronetage; there he found occupation for an idle hour, and consolation in a distressed one; there his faculties were roused into admiration and respect... there any unwelcome sensations arising from domestic affairs, changed naturally into pity and contempt... and there... he could read his own history with an interest which never failed.*

The benefits Sir Walter gained from reading the Baronetage would, in Jane Austen's time, be more commonly expected to be gained from reading the Bible. She is perhaps suggesting that Sir Walter values his ancestry and position in society more than Christianity. His bedrock belief is in who he is, and this continues, even when he is no longer at Kellynch Hall.

When Sir Walter Elliot's rash spending leaves him struggling financially, he accedes to his lawyer's suggestion that he move to Bath and rent out Kellynch Hall, rather than curb his ostentatious lifestyle in the country. His lawyer, Mr Shepherd, suggests that a retired naval officer might be a suitable tenant. Sir Walter's first response is not encouraging:

> *"... it is in two points offensive to me; I have two strong grounds of objection to it. First as being the means of bringing persons of obscure birth into undue distinction, and raising men to honours*

which their fathers and grandfathers never dreamt of; and,
secondly, it cuts up a man's youth and vigour most horribly; a
sailor grows old sooner than any other man; I have observed it all
my life.

Unlike *Mansfield Park*, where a chastened Sir Thomas is allowed by Jane Austen to continue to reside in the ancestral home and lead his family and the estate, in *Persuasion* the rightful owner, Sir Walter Elliot, is removed from Kellynch Hall and Admiral Croft, representing a profession so despised by Sir Walter, is put in residence. *Persuasion* takes Jane's thinking about society one stage further than *Mansfield Park*. In her mind, Sir Walter Elliot no longer deserves Kellynch Hall. So she banishes him. Banishment is another biblical reference – Adam and Eve were banished from the Garden of Eden for their disobedience. Sir Walter does not return to his ancestral home; he is left by Jane Austen in Bath, the acme of transient living, though he is too shallow and worldly-minded to recognize his punishment. Jane Austen's treatment of Sir Walter Elliot is very significant with regard to what we know of her view of society and her respect for the traditional ordering of the social classes. By contrast, it is Admiral and Mrs Croft – he who has worked his way up through the ranks of the Navy, and earned his fortune from prize money, she who is the sister of a curate – who keep the residency of Kellynch Hall. There they carry out their duties to all who live and work in the house and on the estate, exactly as they should.

Jane Austen did not promote radical change in the structures of society and church, because she believed that these structures worked well if each person carried out their Christian duty by living their life with a sense of responsibility, kindliness, and thoughtfulness. When things went wrong, it was not the fault of the social structures or the church, she believed, but of the individuals who had failed to take their moral responsibilities seriously. Through Fanny Price of *Mansfield Park*, she showed that the gentry sometimes needed to be restored to their sense of responsibility. In *Persuasion* she went one stage further and suggested that people like the Crofts could be needed to take the place of the gentry to restore the balance, the harmony, and the mutual responsibilities of society.

At the beginning of *Persuasion*, Anne has outwardly lost her bloom and inwardly lost her hope of love, and yet she lives a life devoid of bitterness, and with such sweetness of temper and service to others. Anne Elliot is a character born out of Jane's "wilderness years" – for surely only a writer who has herself suffered, but who has not given up hope, could create Anne Elliot. We have seen that all of Jane Austen's heroines face loss – but for Anne the loss has lasted the longest, for seven years before the novel begins. It is perhaps no coincidence that Jane set the saddest scenes of her story, when Anne feels at her most estranged from Captain Wentworth, in the autumn months of the dying of the year, and set the scenes of hope, when Anne regains her outward bloom and has the love of her heart restored, in the spring. So the biblical story of death and resurrection is again mirrored in *Persuasion*, all the more strongly, for as the loss is greater so the hope and joy of new life at the end of the novel is greater... and yet *Persuasion* was being written as Jane Austen was herself becoming more and more unwell.

Chapter Eight

Last Days and Legacy, 1817–The Present Day

The previous year, 1816, had been a worrying time for the Austen family, for troubles had fallen upon three of Jane's brothers. Charles had been commanding the *Phoenix* when it was shipwrecked off the coast of Asia Minor. The crew were saved and Charles was acquitted of all blame, but he feared that he would have to wait a long time before getting another ship, leaving him and his family with no income, for with the advent of peace in Europe, following the decisive Battle of Waterloo in 1815, the need for naval ships had greatly declined. Henry's banking business had failed, and he had been declared bankrupt. Several members of the family lost money heavily, though, fortunately for Jane, most of the £600 she had received from her novels was invested elsewhere. Finally, there were concerns for Edward, for some neighbours in Chawton village, who had been expecting to inherit the Hampshire estates of the childless Knight family before they made the decision to adopt him, had taken out a lawsuit against him, which was still not resolved.

As the year had developed, Jane had become increasingly unwell. At the end of May, hoping for a cure, she had gone with Cassandra to Cheltenham to drink the spa water, but this had little effect on her symptoms. From the summer of 1816 onwards, as she was completing *Persuasion*, her condition had grown worse, and references to her declining strength had appeared more and more in her letters. However, as her niece Caroline was to write later, Jane was reluctant to draw too much attention to herself:

> *In my later visits to Chawton Cottage, I remember Aunt Jane used often to lie down after dinner – My Grandmother herself was frequently on the sofa... There was only one sofa in the room – and Aunt Jane laid upon 3 chairs which she arranged for herself – I think she had a pillow but she never looked comfortable – She called it **her** sofa, and even when the **other** was unoccupied, **she** never took it.*"[1]

Although tuberculosis and Hodgkin's disease are now thought to be possibilities, it is most commonly thought that Jane had Addison's disease, a condition which was unrecognized in her time. This disease leads to a loss of function of the adrenal glands, and it is only in recent years that it has been curable with drugs. In Jane's day there would have been no hope of a cure. The sufferer experiences increasing weakness and weight loss, with severe gastro-intestinal pain, pain in the back, and brown patches on the skin. However, the disease has periods of remission, leaving the patient feeling better and hopeful of recovery.

In the New Year of 1817 such a remission occurred, and Jane was duly optimistic, writing to a friend:

> *... I have certainly gained strength through the Winter & am not far from being well; & I think I understand my own case now so much better than I did, as to be able by care to keep off any serious return of illness.*[2]

So confident was Jane in this apparent return of her health that she began a new novel, which we know today as *Sanditon*.

Sanditon

What is most striking about *Sanditon* is that Jane Austen embarked on a completely new context for her novel, for Sanditon is a "young and rising bathing-place" set on the south coast of England, two hours' journey from Hailsham. Though still a small village, Sanditon is developing and growing quickly, and so is a very different setting from the traditional settled villages of most of her other novels. As well as having a very contemporary setting, this was a novel set in very modern times, for the entrepreneurial Mr Parker had named his house Trafalgar House (after the 1805 sea battle), which he now regrets, "for Waterloo is more the thing now". In the few chapters that she completed, Jane reflects on the risks of speculation and development, musing on both what is old and traditional and what is new and up-and-coming – recognizing both the good and the bad in each. So we see two very different families: the Heywoods of the old village of Willingden, who scarcely ever leave their home village, and the Parkers of the newly developing Sanditon; and we see the contrast between the Parkers' old house, a snug-looking place, set in a sheltered dip, "rich in the garden, orchard and meadows which are the best embellishments of such a dwelling", and their new home, high on a cliff, with views over the sea with as yet no shade or gardens, but open and exposed to all the grandeur of the elements.

Given Jane's recent experience of ill health, it is not surprising that *Sanditon* is dominated by the subject of health:

> *He [Mr Parker] held it indeed as certain, that no person could be really well, no person, (however upheld for the present by*

fortuitous aids of exercise and spirits in a semblance of health)
could be really in a state of secure and permanent health without
spending at least six weeks by the sea every year. — The sea air
and sea bathing together were nearly infallible, one or the other of
them being a match for every disorder, of the stomach, the lungs or
the blood; they were anti-spasmodic, anti-pulmonary, anti-septic,
anti-bilious and anti-rheumatic. Nobody could catch cold by the
sea, nobody wanted appetite by the sea, nobody wanted spirits,
nobody wanted strength.

The story opens with a medical incident, for Mr Parker is out on the road searching for a medical man for his new resort when his carriage is abruptly overthrown on a rough lane, leaving him with a sprained ankle. However, opinions are divided in Sanditon about the wisdom of having a doctor resident in the village — Mr Parker thinks it will attract more visitors, but his co-speculator, Lady Dedham, thinks that a doctor only encourages people to fancy themselves ill. Several hypochondriacs are satirically described, including the hyperactive busybody Diana Parker, who claims: "We have consulted physician after physician in vain," and the greedy, self-indulgent Arthur Parker, who claims to survive on "weak cocoa and dry toast", but whom Charlotte Heywood observes discreetly making rich cocoa and surreptitiously loading butter onto his toast. "Certainly, Mr Arthur Parker's enjoyments in invalidism were very different from his sisters' — by no means so spiritualized," writes Jane Austen. This marks her only use of the term, and in this context she uses "spiritualized" in a non-religious, and in a satirical, sense — for the authorial voice of *Sanditon* doubts the genuine invalidism of any of the Parker family. While Arthur uses his supposed ill health as a mask for his physical greed, his sisters elevate theirs so that they have the air of martyrs.

In Charlotte Heywood we see a heroine whose only function seems to be to observe, and she does see beneath the surface of those around her. She has been described as a cipher,[3] a nonentity, for there seems to be no depth to her. The story's other characters appear, thus far, as comic caricatures, leading to the sense that these twelve chapters are more along the lines of the burlesque writing in the *Juvenilia* than written with the interest in virtue and character development of her other adult writing.

Although Jane Austen left no clues about how she planned to develop this novel, we do know that she intended to call it *The Brothers* – presumably after the Parker brothers. Sidney Parker, however, only appears on the penultimate page, so we do not know how Jane was planning to draw him, but possibly, given her proposed title, she was expecting to make the Parkers the leading characters, with Sidney as the main focus of interest and character development, rather than the women characters who were at the heart of all her previous novels.

Another possibility is that, in Jane's weakened state of physical health, deep character formation was now too difficult a task, and so she resorted to the caricature writing of her *Juvenilia*, which she could produce with less effort. Alternatively, her character depictions may have been a conscious, or even subconscious, choice – Jane did not want to create characters whom she would come to love, but whom she knew she might have to abandon if her illness resumed.

There is only one passing reference to a clergyman in these first pages of *Sanditon* – Revd Mr Hanking is a subscriber to the library, which does grade him positively in Jane Austen's estimation. There is as yet no mention of his role in the community – perhaps she was aware that a clergyman might have less scope for influence, for good or for bad, in a modern developing community than in a traditional village. With the absence of a leading clergy figure, and with no clear indication of a character whose virtues and character she will develop, the abandoned manuscript of *Sanditon* leaves us unclear about how she might have developed its theme, spiritual or otherwise.

Jane's Death

By 18 March 1817 the severe symptoms of Jane's illness had returned, and she laid aside the *Sanditon* manuscript for the last time. Two weeks later, her niece visited and was shocked by the deterioration in her condition:

> *She was very pale – her voice was weak and low and there was about her, a general appearance of debility and suffering... She was not equal to the exertion of talking to us, and our visit to the sick room was a very short one – Aunt Cassandra soon taking us away – I do not suppose we stayed a quarter of an hour; and I never saw Aunt Jane again.* [4]

On 27 April Jane made a will. She left it unwitnessed, so perhaps she wrote it without her family's knowledge, not wanting them to know that she realized how ill she was. The will indicated that she left everything to Cassandra, except for two bequests of £50, one to her recently bankrupted brother Henry, who was now ordained. The other £50 was left to Madame Bigeon, who had been Henry's housekeeper in London, where Jane had often stayed.

Her local apothecary, Mr Curtis, advised her to go to stay in Winchester, sixteen miles away, to be cared for by a doctor attached to the Winchester County Hospital. So Jane left Chawton Cottage on 24 May, and settled with Cassandra in lodgings in Winchester, very near to the cathedral. Cassandra remained by her side throughout her last weeks, though other family members made frequent visits. Jane made a point of receiving Holy Communion from her clergymen brothers James and Henry while she had the strength to do so. In her last known letter, written at the end of May, Jane described "my dearest sister" Cassandra as "my tender, watchful, indefatigable nurse" and, she continued, "As to what I owe her, and to the anxious affection of all my beloved family on this occasion, I can only cry over it, and pray to God to bless them more and more."[5]

The symptoms fluctuated but, according to her family, "[h]er sweetness of temper never failed. She was ever considerate and grateful to those who attended on her. At times, when she felt rather better, her playfulness of spirit revived, and she amused them even in their sadness".[6]

On 15 July, just three days before her death, Jane's playfulness of spirit did prevail. It was a very wet St Swithun's[7] Day, and many of the inhabitants of Winchester had gone to watch the local horse races. Jane was aware of the commonly held folklore about St Swithun's Day:

> St Swithun's day if thou dost rain
> For forty days it will remain
> St Swithun's day if thou be fair
> For forty days 'twill rain na mair

Jane dictated her last composition, a poem which teasingly imagined the revenge of St Swithun on those who went to watch racing on a saint's day instead of going to a service in church:

> When Winchester races first took their beginning
> It is said the good people forgot their old Saint
> Not applying at all for the leave of Saint Swithin
> And that William of Wykeham's[8] approval was faint.

The races however were fixed and determin'd
The company came and the Weather was charming
The Lords and the Ladies were sattin'd & ermin'd
And nobody saw any future alarming.

But when the old Saint was informed of these doings
He made but one spring from his shrine to the roof
Of the Palace which now lies so sadly in ruins
And then he address'd them all standing aloof.

Oh, subjects rebellious, Oh Venta[9] depraved
When once we are buried you think we are dead
But behold me Immortal.— By vice you're enslaved
You have sinn'd & must suffer. —Then farther he said

These races & revels & dissolute measures
With which you're debasing a neighbouring Plain
Let them stand — you shall meet with your curse in your pleasures
Set off for your course, I'll pursue with my rain.

Ye cannot but know my command o'er July
Henceforward I'll triumph in shewing my powers,
Shift your race as you will it shall never be dry
The curse upon Venta is July in showers.[10]

That evening the symptoms of Jane's illness returned in force, though now she slept most of the time and appeared to her watching family to be comfortable. After the final seizure, before she lapsed into unconsciousness, Cassandra asked if she wanted anything, and she replied that she wanted nothing but death: "God grant me patience, pray for me, oh, pray for me!"[11] Cassandra was with her when she died in the early hours of 18 July, the sisters as close at Jane's death as they had been in their early childhoods and throughout all of their lives. Immediately after Jane's death, Cassandra wrote to their niece Fanny Knight:

> *I **have** lost a treasure, such a sister, such a friend as never can have been surpassed. She was the sun of my life, the gilder of every pleasure, the soother of every sorrow; I had not a thought concealed from her, and it is as if I had lost a part of myself.*[12]

Jane Austen left a legacy that was more than her writings – for she left her family with profound gratitude for their relationships with her. She did not let her relationships suffer because of her great talent and her family genuinely grieved her loss as their sister and aunt.

The house where Jane Austen lived for her last weeks, 8 College Street, was within the parish of St Swithun. Dying within the parish entitled her to be buried within the precinct of Winchester Cathedral. However, the Austen family asked the cathedral Dean and Chapter if Jane could be buried in the cathedral itself and, to their great satisfaction, their wish was granted. It says something of the high regard of her family for Jane that they chose such a public place for her grave rather than the churchyard at Chawton close to the family home, where her mother and sister would later be buried. After describing her death, Cassandra continued in her letter to Fanny:

> *The last sad ceremony is to take place on Thursday morning; her dear remains are to be deposited in the cathedral. It is a satisfaction to me to think that they are to lie in a building she admired so much; her precious soul, I presume to hope, reposes in a far superior mansion. May mine one day be re-united to it!*[13]

The burial took place early on the morning of Thursday 24 July, and Jane was laid to rest in the north aisle of the cathedral. It was the custom at that time that only men attended funerals, so Cassandra was not present for the service, which was attended by her brothers Edward, Henry, and Frank, and nephew James Edward, James' son.

Memorials to Jane Austen

Henry, in consultation with other members of the family, composed the words for Jane's gravestone:

> *In Memory of JANE AUSTEN youngest daughter of the late REVD GEORGE AUSTEN, formerly Rector of Steventon in this county. She departed this life on the 18th July 1817, aged 41, after a long illness supported with the patience and the hopes of a Christian.*
>
> *The benevolence of her heart, the sweetness of her temper and the extraordinary endowments of her mind obtained the regard of all who knew her, and the warmest love of her intimate connections. Their grief is in proportion to their affection, they know their loss to be irreparable, but in their deepest affection they are consoled by a firm though humble hope that her charity, devotion, faith and purity have rendered her soul acceptable in the sight of her REDEEMER.*

Today's visitors to Winchester Cathedral are often surprised that these words say nothing of Jane Austen's writings. It must be remembered that Jane's identity as the author of her four published novels remained a secret known by few outside the immediate family. Even bearing in mind the context of the high-flown language that was commonly used on memorial stones at the time, the strong emphasis on Jane's virtues, her character, and her Christian faith are marked in Henry's words about her. At the time of her death, the family could have had no idea of the approbation with which she would soon be regarded by the wider world. In 1871, with the proceeds from the publication of his *Memoir of Jane Austen*, which was the first full biography of Jane Austen, her nephew, James Edward Austen-Leigh, paid for an ornate brass plaque to be placed on the wall adjacent to her grave, which bore witness again to her Christian faith and the love of her family, but also acknowledged her writings and her growing fame:

Jane Austen, known to many by her writings, endeared to her family by the very charms of her character and ennobled by Christian faith and piety, was born at Steventon in the County of Hants (sic) Dec 16th 1775 and buried in this Cathedral July 24th 1817. "She openeth her mouth with wisdom and in her tongue is the law of kindness" (Psalm 31 verse 26)[KJV]

Above this tablet there is now a memorial window, which was paid for by public subscription in 1900. The figures depicted are St Augustine of Hippo (or Austin for short, therefore providing a linguistic link with Jane Austen), King David, St John (displaying the first words of his Gospel, "In the beginning was the Word..."), and the four sons of Korah, mentioned in the Old Testament Chronicles, who are traditionally taken to be psalmists. Alongside the psalmists are quotations from the psalms, chosen to reflect Jane's spirituality:

Come, children, hearken to me: I will teach you the fear of the Lord. He will guide the meek in judgement: he will teach the meek his ways.
My mouth shall speak wisdom: and the meditation of my heart understanding.
My mouth shall shew forth thy justice; thy salvation all the day long. Because I have not known learning.[14]

The words of these chosen biblical texts affirm Jane Austen's spirituality with its emphasis on inward reformation and an outward concern for wisdom and justice. It is unfortunate that most of the biblical figures in this window are so obscure, that the biblical words are in Latin, and that the text references are taken from the Vulgate (the Latin Bible), which few people use today. As a result, most visitors to Winchester Cathedral take little notice of this testimony to Jane Austen's spirituality, and the window is little known outside the cathedral.

Jane Austen's Developing Fame

The only published review of any of Jane Austen's novels during her lifetime was a review of *Emma* by the popular author Walter Scott in the March 2016 *Quarterly Review*, which praised Jane's ability in "copying from nature as she really exists in the common walks of life, and presenting to the reader, instead of the splendid scenes of an imaginary world, a correct and striking representation of that which is daily taking place around him".[15] The next published review came four years after her death, from the theologian Richard Whately, writing again in the *Quarterly Review*, who wrote that imaginative literature, when properly done, as exemplified by Jane Austen, concerned itself with generalized human experience from which the reader could gain important insights into human nature. Such writing was moral, he suggested, and he praised Jane Austen's approach:

> *Miss Austen has the merit (in our judgement most essential)*
> *of being evidently a Christian writer: a merit which is much*
> *enhanced, both on the score of good taste, and of practical utility,*
> *by her religion not being at all obtrusive... The moral lessons...*
> *spring incidentally from the circumstances of the story; they are*
> *not forced upon the reader.[16]*

Jane Austen's six completed novels began to be republished in the 1830s, and they have remained continuously in print since then. They were not bestsellers in the Victorian age, when the more sensational writings of Dickens and the Brontës held sway over the literary world. Charlotte Brontë famously criticized the absence of overt passion in Jane Austen's work, describing *Pride and Prejudice* as "a carefully fenced, highly cultivated garden, with neat borders and delicate flowers, but no glance of bright vivid physiognomy, no open country, no fresh air, no blue hill, no bonny beck. I should hardly like to live with her ladies and gentlemen, in their elegant but confined houses."[17] Those who did read and savour Austen saw themselves as a discriminating and cultured few.

However, James Edward Austen-Leigh's *Memoir* of his Aunt Jane, published in 1870, marked the beginning of Jane's rise in popularity and literary acclaim. After this, her novels were translated into other languages, economical editions (the equivalents of today's much cheaper paperbacks) were published, and the illustrated editions and boxed sets of her works first appeared. Frequent critical analyses of her works were now written, and she began to be popular in the United States. As she became more acclaimed at the beginning of the twentieth century, members of the literary elite who savoured her writing began to refer to themselves as Janeites, in order to distinguish themselves from the masses who, in their view, did not properly understand Austen. The cult of Jane Austen was wonderfully portrayed by Rudyard Kipling in his poem *Jane's Marriage*, subtitled *The Janeites*, which was first published in the 1920s:

> *Jane went to Paradise:*
> *That was only fair.*
> *Good Sir Walter followed her,*

And armed her up the stair.
Henry and Tobias,
And Miguel of Spain,
Stood with Shakespeare at the top
To welcome Jane –

Then the Three Archangels
Offered out of hand
Anything in Heaven's gift
That she might command.
Azrael's eyes upon her,
Raphael's wings above,
Michael's sword against her heart,
Jane said: "Love."

Instantly the under-
Standing Seraphim
Laid their fingers on their lips
And went to look for him.
Stole across the Zodiac,
Harnessed Charles's Wain,
And whispered round the Nebulae
"Who loved Jane?"

In a private limbo
Where none had thought to look,
Sat a Hampshire gentleman
Reading of a book.
It was called **Persuasion**
And it told the plain
Story of the love between
Him and Jane.

He heard the question,
Circle Heaven through –
Closed the book and answered: "I did – and do!"
Quietly but speedily
(As Captain Wentworth moved)
Entered into Paradise
The man Jane loved!

By the time of Kipling's poem, Jane Austen's place among internationally known British authors was secure. Her books have remained core texts for schools and universities since then, and they continue to be read in many translations all around the world. The twentieth and twenty-first centuries have seen the publication of countless biographies and other books about her, and a number of organizations have been established to enable her fans to understand more about her life, writings, and times.

The Jane Austen Society was founded in 1940 with the aim of raising funds to purchase Chawton Cottage, where Jane had lived from 1809 to 1817. The cottage was purchased by T. Edward Carpenter in 1947, who vested it in a trust for the benefit of the nation. Jane Austen's House Museum was opened at Chawton Cottage in 1949 by the Jane Austen Memorial Trust, a registered charity which has as its object the advancement of education and in particular the study of English literature, especially the works of Jane Austen. The museum is visited by approximately thirty thousand people each year. As well as supporting the work of the Museum and the Trust, the Jane Austen Society today promotes the appreciation and study of her life, work, and times, through publications and lectures, and secures the preservation of her manuscripts, letters, and memorabilia and those of the Austen family. The Society has branches in several other parts of the world, including the thriving Jane Austen Society of North America.

A Jane Austen Festival is held every September in Bath, based around the Jane Austen Centre at 40 Gay Street, with an appeal to the more popular, less academically focused end of the Jane Austen market. The first festival was held over a weekend in 2001, but fifteen years later the 2016 festival lasted for ten days – testimony to the growing popularity of all things connected to Jane Austen. The focus of the Festival is on entering into her life and times, with opportunities for participants to dress and parade around the city in Regency costume, go to balls, sample food from her era, and enjoy readings and dramatizations of her novels.

Films and Dramatizations

A key development in the growing popularity of Jane Austen has been the film and television dramatizations of her books, beginning with the 1940 film *Pride and Prejudice*, directed by Robert Z. Leonard and starring Greer Garson as Elizabeth Bennet and Laurence Olivier as Darcy. Some of these more recent Jane Austen dramatizations have so taken over the public imagination that it can be difficult to convince people that the picture of Darcy emerging from the lake in the grounds of Pemberley in his wet, body-hugging under-garments, as portrayed by Colin Firth in the 1995 BBC serial of *Pride and Prejudice*, came from the mind of Andrew Davies, who adapted the novel for television, rather than from Jane Austen!

While the dramatizations have done much to bring the wonderful stories of Jane Austen to a wider audience, when looked at from a perspective of spirituality, much is lost when the books are translated onto the screen. One loss is in the passing of time. The self-reflection and character growth that play such an important part in the novels cannot easily be portrayed in a film. Thus the serializations work better than the films or one-episode dramas, especially when watched by the viewer once a week for a period of several weeks, for these enable a much greater sense of the passing of time to be portrayed. This time is needed for characters to ponder, to regret past attitudes and actions, to grow inwardly and, as a result, to change their behaviour. Without this, a film or single-episode dramatization inevitably tends to be driven more by plot than by character development. Thus the 1980 (five-episode) and the 1995 (six-episode) BBC dramatizations of *Pride and Prejudice* are far more satisfying that the 2005 film directed by Joe Wright. An exception to this is *Persuasion* as, in this novel, most of Anne's reflection and character growth has taken place over the seven years between Captain Wentworth's first proposal and the Elliot family's preparing to leave Kellynch Hall, with which the novel begins. The BBC 1995 one-off dramatization of *Persuasion* is excellent and very true to the spirit and the context of Jane's novel, though much of the credit for this must go to actor Amanda Root, for her sensitive portrayal of Anne Elliot.

Jane Austen wrote very much within her own times. Unlike Shakespeare, whose works are sometimes successfully transposed into a different time frame from the Tudor era in which he wrote them, her stories are set within the thought world and values of England in the early nineteenth century. When directors seek to make the story more acceptable to a modern audience, by changing the values of the time in which the novel was set, or substantially changing the plot or the dialogue, the dramatizations can run into difficulties. For example, the director of the 2007 ITV dramatization of *Mansfield Park* chose to make Fanny Price, played by Billie Piper, a much feistier character than was described by Jane Austen, thinking that the modern viewer would find the timid and submissive Fanny unacceptable as a heroine. But the outworking of the plot of *Mansfield Park* demands that Fanny be a submissive and obedient character –

for this makes her refusal to obey Sir Thomas, when she rejects Henry Crawford's offer of marriage, the major watershed of the novel. With a more brazen Fanny, the plot of *Mansfield Park* simply cannot work. Patricia Rozema, director of the 2000 Miramax film *Mansfield Park*, also took a controversial angle in her film by choosing to make a much greater feature of the slave trade than the original novel is able to sustain, thus also skewing the plot to the detriment of its original themes. For a faithful representation of the novel, the 1983 BBC *Mansfield Park* serialization is highly recommended.

The focus on plot in many of the films and dramatizations, to the detriment of attending to the virtues and development of the characters, has led to a much thinner appreciation of what Jane Austen offers us. As a result, for many people today, the appeal of Jane Austen is entirely about romance: the falling in love and the marriages, set within the world of balls and Regency costumes, overlaid with a hazy historical nostalgia. There is much money that can be made in this Jane Austen world! For example, there is an industry in Jane Austen weddings: "Be inspired by the romance of Jane Austen and tell your very own love story with country florals, antique china and, of course, an Elizabeth Bennet-worthy dress,"[18] suggests one such 2016 website. Yet, as we have seen, the only wedding Jane Austen actually described is Emma's, which was said to be, from Mrs Elton's point of view, unfashionable and extremely shoddy. But it was the inner meaning of the marriage service that mattered to Jane Austen, so much more than the outward show of the wedding. As we have seen, it is the deep inner transformation of her leading characters that is the purpose of each of her novels – the wedding was the reward granted to her heroes and heroines for their inner growth and change. It was not the purpose of the story.

Given that Jane Austen disliked Bath when she lived there,

finding it a place that promoted outward show, self-gratification, and superficiality, rather than inward depth, self-improvement, and service to others, I suspect that she would find some of the activities and merchandise that are promoted in her name to be both incomprehensible and trivial. I believe she would be greatly disappointed that the focus on them masks, for many people, the more serious and important themes of much of her writing.[19]

In recent years there has been an outpouring of books of varying literary quality, written as prequels or sequels to her novels, or to develop a Jane Austen theme. Some such writers have gone to extraordinary lengths to be original – such as Seth Grahame-Smith's creation of a zombie horror story, *Pride and Prejudice and Zombies*, where the characters are constantly at war with zombies, who are their deceased ancestors. There is also Karen Joy Fowler's *The Jane Austen Book Club*, in which the six members of a reading group in Sacramento, California each find their life drawn into a parallel with one of the six novels after each of the six book-club meetings. Both these books have been made into very popular films, affirming the success of the ever-expanding industry that the Jane Austen cult has spawned.

The Jane Austen Project, sponsored by the publishing company HarperCollins, has recruited different popular mass-market authors to set the stories of Jane Austen's novels in the present day. These modern retellings do remind us that Jane Austen was herself setting her stories in her own contemporary times, and that she was not writing historical fiction. However, they have come up against the problem that faced the 2007 ITV production of *Mansfield Park*, namely that the values and mores of Jane Austen's day were intrinsic to her plots, making it difficult to make them credible when translated into a different time frame. In Joanna Trollope's 2013 *Sense and Sensibility*, the reason given for Edward's keeping his engagement to Lucy (which in the original is all about being honourable, a virtue whose outworking has changed today) is that he knows that she has been badly hurt in the past and he does not want to hurt her further by breaking the engagement. This is less than convincing, as most of us today would consider that entering a marriage when deeply in love with someone else is a greater cause of hurt than breaking an engagement, and Lucy Steele is not in any way a tender flower.

Val McDermid's *Northanger Abbey* has Cat Moorland obsessed with vampire books, and after some weeks at the Edinburgh Fringe she goes to stay in Northanger Abbey, which is set in the Scottish Borders, where her imagination is fuelled by her vampire obsession, leading her to wonder if the Tilneys are vampires. Again, this does not feel convincing. General Tilney then forces Cat to go home because he has heard from John Thorpe that Cat is a lesbian using a supposed attraction to Henry Tilney as a smokescreen to be near Ellie Tilney, the real source of her passion.

Alexander McCall Smith sets his *Emma* in a Norfolk village, to which Emma has returned after university, unsure of what her future career might be. Though very much further from London than Highbury, the location allows for a stronger sense of provinciality in the twenty-first century than a setting near today's Box Hill would allow. Even so, the reader is left wondering why, in a world of mobile phones and social media, Emma could be so cut off from the rest of the world, and why it is so difficult for Frank Churchill to be in touch with his father.

Curtis Sittenfeld sets her version of *Pride and Prejudice*, *Eligible*, in Cincinnati. In an environment where Elizabeth and Darcy engage in "hate sex" soon after their first meeting, it must have been hard for Sittenfeld to come up with something shocking enough for Lydia to do to horrify and shame her family! Again, the story is not convincing – Lydia elopes with a man who turns out to be transgender, which deeply shocks the prejudiced Mr and Mrs Bennet. However, Darcy, who is a neurosurgeon, helps the family by enabling Mr and Mrs Bennet to understand some of the physiological and psychological issues surrounding transgenderism and, thanks to his intervention, the Bennets are reconciled to Lydia's husband and Lydia is restored to the family.

In seeking to relate to a modern audience, there are few clergy or references to the role of the church in society in these new versions. Many of Jane Austen's clergy, including Mr Collins, have been given other professions but, of those that remain, Cat Moorland's clergyman father and Revd Philip Elton, the non-stipendiary vicar of Highbury, come across as old-fashioned. There is a much stronger emphasis on characters finding self-gratification than there is on their seeking to become better people, developing a sense of service to others, or influencing wider society. The books are considerably shorter and easier to read than the originals, making them much more focused on plot rather than character, and on action rather than self-refection. So, in these modern rewrites, as with many of the films and TV dramatizations, the deeper sense of spirituality of Jane Austen's novels is very much missing.

The production of Jane Austen memorabilia and merchandise and of books and television programmes in 2017, the bicentenary of her death, affirmed her unabated popular appeal. In the same year the national recognition of her significance was confirmed when she first appeared on the Bank of England's ten-pound note, and so her image now passes through the hands of countless millions of people. As Kipling's poem concludes:

Jane lies in Winchester, blessed be her shade!
Praise the Lord for making her, and her for all she made.
And while the stones of Winchester – or Milsom Street – remain,
Glory, Love, and Honour unto England's Jane!

There are all sorts of ways in which people today can enjoy the legacy that Jane Austen has left to the world: watching the screen adaptations of her novels, dancing at a "Jane Austen" Regency ball, going to a lecture or talk that is inspired by her writings, walking "in the footsteps of Jane" in Bath, Hampshire, or Lyme Regis, reading one of the hundreds of books written about her or written as a follow-on to her novels, visiting her home at Chawton Cottage, parading through Bath in Regency costume, attending a "Jane Austen"-style wedding, sampling a "Tea with Mr Darcy" at the Regency Tea Room at Bath's Jane Austen Centre... but the way to get the best from Jane Austen's legacy is to read the novels, and to read them slowly.

There are many lenses through which Jane Austen's novels can be read. Each one will open up her stories and the quality of her writing in a different way. This book has focused on reading her books and considering her life through the lens of spirituality. Jane's spirituality was the outworking of the quiet and measured Anglican faith of her father, which is expressed implicitly rather than explicitly in her novels. This lens has enabled us to explore parallels between her life and her writings, to relish the depth and inner meaning of her writings that point beyond the storyline to deeper principles, and to see her heroines and heroes develop and acquire virtues that enable them to live richer inner lives and improve the lives of others in their communities.

Appendix

Jane Austen's Prayers[1]

I

Give us grace, almighty father, so to pray, as to deserve to be heard, to address thee with our hearts, as with our lips. Thou art everywhere present, from thee no secret can be hid. May the knowledge of this, teach us to fix our thoughts on thee, with reverence and devotion that we pray not in vain.

Look with mercy on the sins we have this day committed and in mercy make us feel them deeply, that our repentance may be sincere, & our resolution steadfast of endeavouring against the commission of such in future. Teach us to understand the sinfulness of our own hearts, and bring to our knowledge every fault of temper and every evil habit in which we have indulged to the discomfort of our fellow-creatures, and the danger of our own souls. May we now, and on each return of night, consider how the past day has been spent by us, what have been our prevailing thoughts, words and actions during it, and how far we can acquit ourselves of evil. Have we thought irreverently of thee, have we disobeyed thy commandments, have we neglected any known duty, or willingly given pain to any human being? Incline us to ask our hearts these questions oh! God, and save us from deceiving ourselves by pride or vanity.

Give us a thankful sense of the blessings in which we live, of the many comforts of our lot; that we may not deserve to lose them by discontent or indifference.

Be gracious to our necessities, and guard us, and all we love, from evil this night. May the sick and afflicted, be now, and ever thy care; and heartily do we pray for the safety of all that travel by land or by sea, for the comfort & protection of the orphan and widow and that thy pity may be shown upon all captives and prisoners.

Above all other blessings oh! God, for ourselves and our fellow-creatures, we implore thee to quicken our sense of thy mercy in the redemption of the world, of the value of that holy religion in which we have been brought up, that we may not, by our own neglect, throw away the salvation thou hast given us, nor be Christians only in name. Hear us almighty God, for his sake who has redeemed us, and taught us thus to pray. Our Father which art in heaven &c.

II

Almighty God! Look down with mercy on thy servants here assembled and accept the petitions now offered up unto thee. Pardon oh! God the offences of the past day. We are conscious of many frailties; we remember with shame and contrition, many evil thoughts and neglected duties; and we have perhaps sinned against thee and against our fellow-creatures in many instances of which we have no remembrance. Pardon oh God! whatever thou hast seen amiss in us, and give us a stronger desire of resisting every evil inclination and weakening every habit of sin. Thou knowest the infirmity of our nature, and the infirmities which surround us.

Be thou merciful oh heavenly Father! to creatures so formed and situated. We bless thee for every comfort of our past and present existence, for our health of body and of mind and for every other source of happiness which thou hast bountifully bestowed on us and with which we close this day, imploring their continuance from thy fatherly goodness, with a more grateful sense of them, than they have hitherto excited. May the comforts of every day, be thankfully felt by us, may they prompt a willing obedience of thy commandments and a benevolent spirit toward every fellow-creature.

Have mercy oh gracious Father! upon all that are now suffering from whatever cause, that are in any circumstance of danger or distress. Give them patience under every affliction, strengthen, comfort and relieve them.

To thy goodness we commend ourselves this night beseeching thy protection of us through its darkness and dangers. We are helpless and dependent; graciously preserve us. For all whom we love and value, for every friend and connection, we equally pray; however divided and far asunder, we know that we are alike before thee, and under thine eye. May we be equally united in thy faith and fear, in fervent devotion towards thee, and in thy merciful protection this night. Pardon oh Lord! the imperfections of these our prayers, and accept them through the mediation of our blessed saviour, in whose holy words, we further address thee; our Father &c.

III

Father of heaven! whose goodness has brought us in safety to the close of this day, dispose our hearts in fervent prayer. Another day is now gone, and added to those, for which we were before accountable. Teach us almighty father, to consider this solemn truth, as we should do, that we may feel the importance of every day, and every hour as it passes, and earnestly strive to make a better use of what thy goodness may yet bestow on us, than we have done of the time past.

Give us grace to endeavour after a truly Christian spirit to seek to attain that temper of forbearance and patience of which our blessed saviour has set us the highest example; and which, while it prepares us for the spiritual happiness of the life to come, will secure to us the best enjoyment of what this world can give. Incline us Oh God! to think humbly of ourselves, to be severe only in the examination of our own conduct, to consider our fellow-creatures with kindness, and to judge all they say and do with that charity which we would desire from them ourselves.

We thank thee with all our hearts for every gracious dispensation, for all the blessings that have attended our lives, for every hour of safety, health and peace, of domestic comfort and innocent enjoyment. We feel that we have been blessed far beyond any thing that we have deserved; and though we cannot but pray for a continuance of all these mercies, we acknowledge our unworthiness of them and implore thee to pardon the presumption of our desires.

Keep us oh! Heavenly Father from evil this night. Bring us in safety to the beginning of another day and grant that we may rise again with every serious and religious feeling which now directs us.

May thy mercy be extended over all mankind, bringing the ignorant to the knowledge of thy truth, awakening the impenitent, touching the hardened. Look with compassion upon the afflicted of every condition, assuage the pangs of disease, comfort the broken in spirit.

More particularly we do pray for the safety and welfare of our own family and friends wheresoever dispersed, beseeching thee to avert from them all material and lasting evil of body and mind; and may we by the assistance of thy holy spirit so conduct ourselves on earth as to secure an eternity of happiness with each other in thy heavenly kingdom. Grant this most merciful Father, for the sake of our blessed saviour in whose holy name and words we further address thee. Our Father which art in heaven &c.

NOTES

Introduction: Jane Austen – A Spiritual Writer?

1. J. E. Austen-Leigh, *A Memoir of Jane Austen and Other Family Recollections* (Oxford: Oxford University Press, 2002), pp. 79–80 (italics are in the text).
2. Michael Wheeler, "Religion", in Janet Todd (ed.), *Jane Austen in Context* (Cambridge: Cambridge University Press, 2005), pp. 406–14.

Chapter One: Early Influences, 1775–86

1. Deirdre Le Faye (ed.), *Jane Austen: A Family Record* (London: The British Library, 1989), p. 24.
2. E.g. Claire Tomalin, *Jane Austen: A Life* (London: Viking, 1997), pp. 5–7.
3. Referring to a visit to Mr Fitzhugh, who was so deaf that Jane thought he wouldn't be able to hear a cannon if it was fired close to home. She describes herself as having "talked to him a little with my fingers…" (Letter to Cassandra Austen, 27–28 December 1808 in *Jane Austen's Letters*, Brabourne Edition, 1984).
4. Anna Lefroy in J. E. Austen-Leigh, *A Memoir of Jane Austen and Other Family Recollections*, p. 160.
5. See Deidre Le Faye (ed.), *Jane Austen: A Family Record*, p. 3.
6. For example, the Austens did not give any of their six sons the first name Thomas, as they might have done if they had felt that they needed to show obsequious gratitude to their patron, Thomas Knight. Only their fourth son, Henry, had Thomas as his second name. We can conjecture that the fictional Mr Collins of *Pride and Prejudice* would insist

on naming his forthcoming child after a member of the de Bourgh family.

7. Henry Austen, *Biographical Notice of the Author (1818)*, in J. E. Austen-Leigh, *A Memoir of Jane Austen and Other Family Recollections*, p. 137.

8. Letter to Francis Austen, 21 January 1805, Letter 40 in Deirdre Le Faye (ed.), *Jane Austen's Letters* (Oxford: Oxford University Press, 2011 [Fourth Edition]), p. 100.

9. Letter to Francis Austen, 22 January 1805, Letter 41 in Deirdre Le Faye (ed.), *Jane Austen's Letters*, p. 101.

10. Ibid.

11. Thomas Keymer's essay "Rank" in *Jane Austen in Context* informs us that in England in 1803 there were 540 baronets, 350 knights, 6,000 landed squires, and 20,000 gentlemen, making up 1.4% of the national population. "It is to this rurally based society, centred on major land owning families and descending in fine graduations through non-landed professionals and moneyed rentiers of varying status, that Austen's characters refer when they speak of 'the neighbourhood'."

12. Letter to Anna Austen, 9 September 1814 in *Jane Austen's Letters*, Brabourne Edition.

13. Deirdre Le Faye (ed.), *Jane Austen: A Family Record*, p. 50.

14. Letter to Cassandra Austen, 23 June 1814 in *Jane Austen's Letters*, Brabourne Edition.

15. Constance Hill, *Jane Austen: Her Homes and Her Friends*, (London and New York: John Lane, 1923), pp. 48–49, taken from George Holbert Tucker, *A Goodly Heritage: A History of Jane Austen's Family* (Stroud: Sutton Publishing Ltd, 1998), p. 133.

16. In describing the visit of a little girl, Jane wrote: "Our little visitor has just left us, and left us highly pleased with her; she is a nice, natural, open-hearted, affectionate girl, with

all the ready civility which one sees in the best children in the present day; so unlike anything that I was myself at her age, that I am often all astonishment and shame" (Letter to Cassandra Austen, 8–9 February 1807 in *Jane Austen's Letters*, Brabourne Edition).

17. Deirdre Le Faye (ed.), *Jane Austen: A Family Record*, p. 49.
18. Letter to Cassandra, 8–11 April 1805, Letter 43 in Deirdre Le Faye (ed.), *Jane Austen's Letters*, p. 105.
19. Karl Moritz, *Travels in England in 1782*, Chapter Four, www.visionofbritain.org.uk/travellers/Moritz.
20. J. E. Austen-Leigh, *A Memoir of Jane Austen and Other Family Recollections*, p. 11.
21. Andrew Gant, *O Sing unto the Lord: A History of English Church Music* (London: Profile Books, 2015), p. 249.
22. J. H. and E. C. Hubback, *Jane Austen's Sailor Brothers* (London and New York: John Lane, 1906), p. 17, taken from George Holbert Tucker, *A Goodly Heritage: A History of Jane Austen's Family*, p. 167.

Chapter Two: The Development of the Writer, 1787–1800

1. Letter to Cassandra Austen, 18 December 1798 in *Jane Austen's Letters*, Brabourne Edition.
2. E.g.:
THE BEAUTIFUL CASSANDRA
A NOVEL IN TWELVE CHAPTERS
"dedicated by permission to Miss Austen.
Dedication.
MADAM
You are a Phoenix. Your taste is refined, your Sentiments are noble, & your Virtues innumerable. Your Person is lovely, your Figure, elegant, & your Form, majestic. Your Manners are polished, your Conversation is rational & your

appearance singular. If therefore the following Tale will afford one moment's amusement to you, every wish will be gratified of

Your most obedient humble servant

THE AUTHOR"

(R. W. Chapman [ed.], *Minor Works* [Oxford: Oxford University Press, 1989], p. 44)

THE VISIT

A COMEDY IN 2 ACTS

"Dedication

To the Revd James Austen

SIR,

The following Drama, which I humble recommend to your Protection & Patronage. tho' inferior to those celebrated Comedies called 'The School for Jealousy' & 'The travelled Man', will I hope afford some amusement to so respectable a Curate as yourself; which was the end in veiw (*sic*) when it was first composed by your Humble Servant the Author".

(R. W. Chapman [ed.], *Minor Works*, p. 49)

3. Letter to Cassandra Austen, 27–28 October 1798 in *Jane Austen's Letters*, Brabourne Edition.

4. Letter to Cassandra Austen, 8–9 February 1807 in *Jane Austen's Letters*, Brabourne Edition.

5. Letter to Cassandra Austen, 30 January 1809 in *Jane Austen's Letters*, Brabourne Edition.

6. Letter to Cassandra Austen, 8–9 January 1799 in *Jane Austen's Letters*, Brabourne Edition.

7. Letter to Francis Austen, 25 September 1813, Letter 90 in Deirdre Le Faye (ed.), *Jane Austen's Letters*, p. 240.

8. Letter to Cassandra Austen, 8–9 January 1799 in *Jane Austen's Letters*, Brabourne Edition.

9. Letter to Cassandra Austen, 21–23 January 1799 in *Jane Austen's Letters*, Brabourne Edition.

10. Visits to clergy included a visit to Revd Thomas Leigh, the Rector of Adlestrop in Gloucestershire, in 1794, and frequent visits to her godfather, Revd Samuel Cooke, at Great Bookham in Surrey.

11. Letter to Cassandra Austen, 9–10 January 1796 in *Jane Austen's Letters*, Brabourne Edition.

12. Deirdre Le Faye (ed.), *Jane Austen: A Family Record*, p. 94: "Cassandra's lot in life did indeed turn out to be spinsterhood; without in any way becoming a melancholy recluse, she evidently felt that no other man could replace Tom in her affections, so that although she continued to take her place in society and go to dances with Jane, the family gradually came to realise that she preferred to stay single."

13. When writing to Cassandra about the response of various family friends to *Pride and Prejudice*, Jane writes: "And Mr. Hastings! I am quite delighted with what such a man writes about it. Henry sent him the books after his return from Daylesford, but you will hear the letter too." (Letter to Cassandra Austen, 15–16 September 1813 in *Jane Austen's Letters*, Brabourne Edition.)

    Such words suggest that the family had kept a close connection to Warren Hastings.

14. As exemplified in Edmund Burke's *Reflections on the Revolution in France*, published in 1790. The historian J. H. Plumb writes: "His denunciation of revolutionary change... was immensely successful in Tory, as well as in some Whig circles, for it clarified in lucid language the fears and suspicions long felt towards radicalism by those with a large share in the ancient order of things." (J. H. Plumb, *England in the Eighteenth Century (1714 – 1815)* [London: Penguin, 1961], p. 156.)

15. For example, Thomas Paine's widely acclaimed *Rights of Man*, written in 1791 as a defence of the French Revolution against its critics, and as a critique of Edmund Burke's

Reflections on the Revolution in France. Rights of Man concludes by proposing practical reformations of English government: a written constitution composed by a national assembly; the elimination of aristocratic titles; a national budget without allotted military and war expenses; lower taxes for the poor, and subsidized education for them; and a progressive income tax weighted against wealthy estates to prevent the emergence of a hereditary aristocracy.

16. "Burke had extolled the Church of England as the source and sanction on social stability, and so it was. What was going on made churchmen more averse than ever to change. Bishops rivalled one another in denouncing subversive teaching, the spirit of democracy, and the blasphemous character of the revolutionary movement. The effect of the French revolution in England was therefore to strengthen the forces of conservatism and to set the clock back." (Alec R. Vidler, *The Church in an Age of Revolution* [London: Penguin, 1990], p. 34.)

17. A novel is a long narrative, normally in prose, which describes fictional characters and events, usually in the form of a sequential story. Research by the English Short Title Catalogue shows that the yearly output of fiction in English rose exponentially in the last twenty years of the eighteenth century, from about sixty works of fiction published in 1780 to about 130 in 1799. Literary critics such as Ian Watt, who wrote *The Rise of the Novel*, generally see Daniel Defoe's *Robinson Crusoe* (1719) and *Moll Flanders* (1722) as being the first English novels, though there are earlier contenders such as John Bunyan's *Pilgrim's Progress* (1678). Reasons for the rapid increase in novel writing and reading include the rise of the professional middle classes during the eighteenth century, the ease of obtaining books through circulating libraries (the first library was opened in England in 1728),

and, towards the end of the century, the evolution of the Gothic and Romantic Sentimental genres, which had a particular appeal to women.

18. James Fordyce, *Sermons to Young Women* (1766); see www.janeaustensworld.wordpress.com/tag/james-fordyce.

Chapter Three: The Early Novels: *Sense and Sensibility, Pride and Prejudice,* and *Northanger Abbey*

1. In his book *After Virtue*, first published in 1985, Alasdair MacIntyre speaks of a virtue-based approach to morality and ethics which dates back to Aristotle, the Greek philosopher who lived three hundred and fifty years before Christ. This way of approaching ethical issues through the development of the virtues, MacIntyre argues, is crucial in both the teaching of the New Testament and the development of Christian thought throughout the medieval period, but began to deteriorate with the Enlightenment. He claims that Jane Austen was the last significant proponent of virtue in her novels for, under the influence of the Romantic Movement, nineteenth-century novelists were focusing on the passions rather than the virtues and, in the philosophical world, moral thinking was focusing on obeying the rules rather than acquiring virtues (MacIntyre, p. 274).

In the modern understanding, virtues are often, unhelpfully, coupled with particular vices, suggesting that a virtue is simply the opposite of a vice. Aristotle had a much richer understanding. He taught that a virtue is not a fixed entity but a balance, or the mathematical mean, between an excess and a deficiency of the virtue. So courage, according to Aristotle, lies between its excess, recklessness, and its deficiency, cowardice. What courage means in itself cannot be defined, for in any given situation we need judgment to determine what is courageous, what is the right balance between recklessness and cowardice. Similarly, generosity, Aristotle suggests, is the mean between profligacy and meanness in any particular situation.

With this understanding, it is a person's character that will guide them to act well, to find the right balance or mean in each situation, whatever the circumstances might be. So the formation of a person's character is of critical importance, for the habits developed in the past will determine whether or not that person responds in the right way at a time of crisis. When you are young you have to learn what it is to be a good person, and most of us need to be taught by our parents and teachers how to be polite, helpful, and generous to others. We have to consciously work at ways of developing good habits so that we learn to make right judgments and behave in ways that are virtuous. Or it may be that a time of crisis in our lives leads us to reassess our behaviour and recognize that we need to deliberately change some of our habitual ways of living. If we do so, then as we get older virtuous actions flow from our dispositions and become our habit, leading us to behave well in new or in crisis situations.

Jane Austen's approach to virtue is considered in more depth in Sarah Emsley's *Jane Austen's Philosophy of the Virtues*. Emsley examines how Jane Austen explores both the classical virtues, such as prudence, justice, fortitude, and temperance, and the specifically Christian virtues of charity, faith, and love. She shows how Jane Austen depicts in her novels the tensions that arise when different virtues must be practised simultaneously, and the difficulties of competing virtues.

Chapter Four: The Wilderness Years, 1801–09

1. Deirdre Le Faye (ed.), *Jane Austen: A Family Record*, p. 113.
2. Caroline Austen, *My Aunt Jane Austen: A Memoir* (Winchester: Jane Austen Society, 1991) in J. E. Austen-Leigh, *A Memoir of Jane Austen and Other Family Recollections*, p. 174.
3. Letter to Cassandra Austen, 25 January 1801 in *Jane Austen's Letters*, Brabourne Edition.
4. Letter to Cassandra Austen, 21–23 January 1799 in *Jane Austen's Letters*, Brabourne Edition.
5. Letter to Cassandra Austen, 21–22 January 1801 in *Jane Austen's Letters*, Brabourne Edition.
6. Letter to Cassandra Austen, 5–6 May 1801 in *Jane Austen's Letters*, Brabourne Edition.
7. Letter to Cassandra Austen, 2 June 1799 in *Jane Austen's Letters*, Brabourne Edition.
8. Letter to Cassandra Austen, 12–13 May 1801 in *Jane Austen's Letters*, Brabourne Edition.
9. Letter to Cassandra Austen, 21–22 May 1801 in *Jane Austen's Letters*, Brabourne Edition.
10. Ibid.
11. Claire Tomalin, *Jane Austen: A Life*, p. 179.
12. Deirdre Le Faye (ed.), *Jane Austen: A Family Record*, pp. 121–22.
13. Letter to Cassandra Austen, 12–13 May 1801 in *Jane Austen's Letters*, Brabourne Edition.
14. Letter to Cassandra Austen, 8–11 April 1805, Letter 43, in Deirdre Le Faye (ed.), *Jane Austen's Letters*, p. 103.
15. Letter to Cassandra Austen, 21–22 May 1801 in *Jane Austen's Letters*, Brabourne Edition.
16. Letter to Cassandra Austen, 11 June 1799 in *Jane Austen's Letters*, Brabourne Edition.
17. Margaret Drabble (ed.) *Lady Susan, The Watsons, Sanditon* (London: Penguin, 1974), pp. 16–17.

18. Letter to Francis Austen, 21 January 1805, Letter 40, in Deirdre Le Faye (ed.), *Jane Austen's Letters*, p. 100.
19. Ibid.
20. Letter to Cassandra Austen, 8–9 February 1807, Letter 50, in Deirdre Le Faye (ed.), *Jane Austen's Letters*, p. 126.
21. Deirdre Le Faye (ed.), *Jane Austen: A Family Record*, p. 153, quoted from Letter from Richard Cosby, 8 April 1809, Letter 68A, in Deirdre Le Faye (ed.), *Jane Austen's Letters*, p. 183.
22. Letter to Cassandra Austen, 13 October 1808 in *Jane Austen's Letters*, Brabourne Edition.
23. Letter to Cassandra Austen, 24–25 October 1808 in *Jane Austen's Letters*, Brabourne Edition.

Chapter Five: The Chawton Years, 1809–16

1. J. E. Austen-Leigh, *A Memoir of Jane Austen and Other Family Recollections*, pp. 80–81.
2. Constance Hill, *Jane Austen: Her Homes and Her Friends*, p. 202.
3. Letter to Cassandra Austen, 9 December 1808 in *Jane Austen's Letters*, Brabourne Edition.
4. Letter to Martha Lloyd, 29–30 November 1812, Letter 77, in Deirdre Le Faye (ed.), *Jane Austen's Letters*, p. 205.
5. Anna Lefroy in J. E. Austen-Leigh, *A Memoir of Jane Austen and Other Family Recollections*, p. 160.
6. Letter to Cassandra Austen, 24 January 1809 in *Jane Austen's Letters*, Brabourne Edition.
7. Letter to Cassandra Austen, 30 January 1809 in *Jane Austen's Letters*, Brabourne Edition.
8. Jane Austen's novels, particularly *Mansfield Park*, show that she would have concurred with Hannah More on many of the themes of More's other writings, including the value of education for girls that stressed the gaining of virtue not

just the gaining of accomplishments, and the significant influence for good that women could play in their roles as wives and mothers. Where Jane Austen and Hannah More differed enormously was in the way that they expressed their response to their desire for change in society. Hannah More's response was through ardent preaching, teaching, the writing of her evangelistically didactic novel, and her unceasing activity among the poor of the county of Somerset. Jane Austen's response was through the influence of her life and novels, and the use of much less overtly religious language.

9. Henry Austen, *Biographical Notice of the Author (1818)*, in J. E. Austen-Leigh, *A Memoir of Jane Austen and Other Family Recollections*, p. 153.

10. David Cecil, *A Portrait of Jane Austen*, (Harmondsworth: Penguin, 1978), p. 50.

11. To her niece Anna Austen, Jane wrote: "I am very fond of Sherlock's sermons and prefer them to almost any" (Letter to Anna Austen, 28 September 1814 in *Jane Austen's Letters*, Brabourne Edition). Thomas Sherlock was a mid-eighteenth-century Church of England bishop, whose sermons were still widely read in the early nineteenth century.

12. Michael Wheeler, "Religion", in Janet Todd (ed.), *Jane Austen in Context*, p. 411.

13. Letter to Cassandra Austen, 11–12 October, 1813 in *Jane Austen's Letters*, Brabourne Edition.

14. Letter to Cassandra Austen, 26–27 May 1801, Letter 38, in Deirdre Le Faye (ed.), *Jane Austen's Letters*, p. 95.

15. Paula Byrne, *The Real Jane Austen* (London: William Collins, 2013), p. 238.

16. Letter to Cassandra Austen, 11–12 October 1813 in *Jane Austen's Letters*, Brabourne Edition.

17. Letter to Fanny Knight, 18–20 November in *Jane Austen's Letters*, Brabourne Edition.

18. Letter to Fanny Knight, 18–20 November in *Jane Austen's Letters*, Brabourne Edition.

19. Letter to Fanny Knight, 30 November 1814 in *Jane Austen's Letters*, Brabourne Edition.

20. Irene Collins, *Jane Austen and the Clergy* (London: The Hambledon Press, 2002), p. 44.

21. Letter to Cassandra Austen, 15–16 October 1808 in *Jane Austen's Letters*, Brabourne Edition.

22. Letter to Cassandra Austen, 17–18 January 1809 in *Jane Austen's Letters*, Brabourne Edition.

23 Letter to Cassandra Austen, 8–9 September 1816 in *Jane Austen's Letters*, Brabourne Edition.

There is a historic context to Jane's comment about the Bible Society. In 1804 Evangelicals within the Church of England had joined forces with their nonconformist friends to establish the British and Foreign Bible Society, whose single purpose was to distribute Bibles worldwide, without any additional commentary or guide. This was a significantly different approach from that of the long-established SPCK (the Society for Promoting Christian Knowledge), which distributed a wide variety of literature including Bibles and prayer books. There was a powerful public movement against the Bible Society in favour of SPCK's approach, believing that SPCK would better help the recipients of their Christian literature to know how to interpret the Scriptures appropriately.

24. Letter to Fanny Knight, 13 March 1817, Letter 153, in Deirdre Le Faye (ed.), *Jane Austen's Letters*, p. 349.

Chapter Six: The Later Novels: *Mansfield Park*

1. Jane is referring to the so-called "War of 1812", a military conflict between America and the United Kingdom, which lasted from June 1812 until February 1815.
2. Letter to Martha Lloyd, 2 September 2014, Letter 106, in Deirdre Le Faye (ed.), *Jane Austen's Letters*, p. 285.
3. Letter to Francis Austen, 3–6 July 1813, Letter 86, in Deirdre Le Faye (ed.), *Jane Austen's Letters*, p. 226.
4. Edward Said, *Culture and Imperialism* (London: Vintage, 1993), p. 107.
5. Edward Said, *Culture and Imperialism*, p. 115.
6. Ibid.
7. William Wilberforce was a very influential figure during Jane Austen's lifetime though he is not mentioned in any of her extant letters. In 1787, dismayed at the debauchery he observed in society, Wilberforce used his influence as a philanthropist and Member of Parliament to try to ensure tighter enforcement of laws governing public behaviour. He then came to the conclusion that neither manners nor morals could be effective without the religious beliefs that lay at their foundation, and in 1797 he published a widely read tract critiquing the society of the time: *A Practical View of the Prevailing Religious System of Professed Christians, in the Higher and Middle Classes in this Century, Contrasted with Real Christianity*. Jane Austen's writings show that she saw many of the same faults in society that were addressed by him. By the beginning of the nineteenth century, Wilberforce had turned most of his time and attention to his campaign to abolish the slave trade. He stayed at the Sydney Gardens end of Great Pulteney Street in Bath for a few months in 1802, just a few doors away from the Austen family home at 4 Sydney Gardens. Wilberforce's record in his journal of

his stay in the previous year indicates that his presence was very publicly known, for he was "molested with callers and calling". There are no letters from Jane in existence today from 1802, so we can only speculate on how much she was aware of his presence nearby.

8. Paula Byrne, *The Real Jane Austen*, pp. 215–16, 222–23.

9. In 1772, Mansfield declared that James Somerset, an escaped slave living in England, could not be forcibly returned abroad, and that he must be discharged. In 1781, the owners of the *Zong*, a Liverpool slaving ship, filed for compensation for lost cargo after nearly 150 of the captives, sick African men, women, and children, had been thrown overboard. Mansfield ruled that the owners could not claim compensation.

10. Tony Tanner, "Introduction", in *Mansfield Park* (London: Penguin English Library, 1966), p. 8.

11. Tony Tanner, "Introduction", in *Mansfield Park*, pp. 31–32.

12. Alasdair MacIntyre, *After Virtue: A Study in Moral Theology* (London: Bloomsbury, 2007 [Third Edition]), p. 281.

13. In *Westminster Abbey*, Richard Jenkyns points out that while today the nation sees Westminster Abbey "as primarily a place of memory and public ritual... in the past, when it was emptier and dingier, it was seen pre-eminently as a place of death" (Jenkyns, p. 124). Until the twentieth century few national occasions were celebrated at the abbey – for example, no royal weddings were held there between the wedding of Richard II to Anne of Bohemia in 1382 and the wedding of Princess Patricia of Connaught (granddaughter of Queen Victoria) to Alexander Ramsay in 1919. It was of course the location for coronations, but there was no coronation service in Jane's lifetime as she lived her entire life within the reign of George III (and the regency of his son). What the abbey contained in profusion were

memorials, not just to royalty and the great and good, but to others who could afford to place a memorial there. This suggests that Jane Austen did not envisage Dr Grant's move from Mansfield to a canon's stall at Westminster Abbey as being a move to an influential position within the national church, as would be implied by such a move today.

14. David Bebbington, the author of *Evangelicalism in Modern Britain*, maintains that the four distinctive marks of Evangelicalism from the eighteenth century to the present day are: conversion, the belief that lives need to be changed through an experience of conversion through personal faith, resulting in a confident assurance of salvation; biblicism, a particular regard for the Bible and the importance of personal Bible devotions; crucicentrism, a stress on the sacrifice of Christ on the cross; and activism, the expression of the gospel in acts of service to others. These four aspects have remained consistently distinctive marks of Evangelicalism through the three centuries since the beginning of the Evangelical Revival, Bebbington argues, though the emphasis has changed in different cultural periods. These changing emphases partly account for the differing ways in which people use the word "evangelical". During the mid-eighteenth-century beginnings of the Evangelical Revival, the main emphases of the movement were on the first and fourth marks: conversion and crucicentrism. However, in the early part of the nineteenth century, the activities of William Wilberforce and the Clapham Sect drew people's attention more to the activism aspect of Evangelicalism. Until the mid-nineteenth century the centrality of the Bible could still be taken as read, but as biblical criticism developed in the late nineteenth century (for the first time examining biblical texts by using the tools of literary and scientific enquiry), the biblicism aspect of Evangelicalism

came to be more emphasized, leading to a more literal reading of the Bible text by Evangelicals as a counter to the more liberal reading engendered by biblical criticism. Much of Jane's understanding of the importance of moral reform and the need for spiritual influence, particularly in the attitude and behaviour of the clergy, which is such a distinctive theme in *Mansfield Park*, concurs with the activism emphasis of Evangelicalism. It has to be in this area only that we can apply Jane's comment "I am by no means convinced that we ought not all to be evangelicals"; we find nothing in her writings or in the testimony of her family to suggest that her faith had a stronger focus on conversion, biblicism, or crucicentrism than were implicit in her traditional Anglicanism.

15. R. W. Chapman (ed.), *Minor Works*, p. 433.

Chapter Seven: The Later Novels: *Emma* and *Persuasion*

1. J. E. Austen-Leigh, *A Memoir of Jane Austen and Other Family Recollections*, p. 119.

2. "The narration follows the path of Emma's errors. Indeed, the first-time reader will sometimes follow this path too, and then share the heroine's surprise when the truth rushes upon her. Yet it is still a third-person narrative; Emma is not telling her own story. We both share her judgements and watch her making them. Austen was the first novelist to manage this alchemy… It was only in the early 20th century that critics began agreeing on a name for it: free indirect style…" John Mullan, Professor of English, University College, London, in *Guardian Review*, 5 December 2015; www.theguardian.com/books/2015/dec/05/jane-austen-emma-changed-face-fiction.

3. R. W. Chapman (ed.), *Minor Works*, p. 318.

4.   Letter from James Stanier Clarke, 21 December 1815, Letter 132A, in Deirdre Le Faye (ed.), *Jane Austen's Letters*, p. 320.

5.   Letter to James Stanier Clarke, 1 April 1816 in *Jane Austen's Letters*, Brabourne Edition.

6.   R. W. Chapman (ed.), *Minor Works*, pp. 428–30.

7.   Letter to Fanny Knight, 30 November 1814 in *Jane Austen's Letters*, Brabourne Edition.

8.   Ibid.

9.   Deirdre Le Faye (ed.), *Jane Austen: A Family Record*, p. 233.

Chapter 8: Last Days and Legacy, 1817–The Present Day

1.   J. E. Austen-Leigh, *A Memoir of Jane Austen and Other Family Recollections*, p. 177.

2.   Letter to Althea Bigg, Letter 150C, in Deirdre Le Faye (ed.), *Jane Austen's Letters*, p. 341.

3.   Margaret Drabble (ed.), *Lady Susan, The Watsons, Sanditon*, p. 25.

4.   Caroline Austen, *My Aunt Jane Austen: A Memoir* in J. E. Austen-Leigh, *A Memoir of Jane Austen and Other Family Recollections*, p. 179.

5.   Letter to Frances Tilson, Letter 161C, in Deirdre Le Faye (ed.), *Jane Austen's Letters*, p. 358.

6.   Caroline Austen, *My Aunt Jane Austen: A Memoir* in J. E. Austen-Leigh, *A Memoir of Jane Austen and Other Family Recollections*, p. 130.

7.   St Swithun (often spelt Swithin, which is the spelling Jane Austen uses) was a ninth-century bishop of Winchester. He died on 2 July 862 and tradition has it that he asked to be buried in a humble manner, outside Winchester Cathedral in the surrounding precincts. His original grave was situated just outside the west door of the Old Saxon minster, meaning people would inevitably walk over it on their way into the

cathedral. However, on 15 July 971, Swithun's remains were dug up and moved to a shrine in the cathedral on the orders of the current bishop, Ethelwold. This became the saint's day because miracles were attributed to him on this day. However, the removal of Swithun's remains into the cathedral was also accompanied by ferocious and violent rainstorms that lasted forty days and forty nights. People (rightly or wrongly) attributed this to the fact that the saint was obviously angry at being moved. This is probably the origin of the legend that if it rains on St Swithin's feast day, the rain will continue for forty more days.

8. William of Wykeham was a fourteenth-century Bishop of Winchester and Chancellor of England. He founded Winchester College.

9. "Venta" is the Roman name for Winchester.

10. R. W. Chapman (ed.), *Minor Works*, pp. 451–52.

11. Letter from Cassandra Austen to Fanny Knight, 20 July 1817 in *Jane Austen's Letters*, Brabourne Edition.

12. Ibid.

13. Ibid.

14. The texts are taken from the Latin Vulgate Bible , and are numbered from the Vulgate: Psalm 33:12, Psalm 24:9, Psalm 48:4, Psalm 70:15.

15. Deirdre Le Faye (ed.), *Jane Austen: A Family Record*, p. 209.

16. Paula Byrne, *The Real Jane Austen*, pp. 203–204, quoted in Brian Southam (ed.), *Jane Austen: The Critical Heritage* (London: Routledge & Kegan Paul, 1968), p. 95.

17. Quoted in Elizabeth Gaskell, *The Life of Charlotte Brontë* (Oxford: Oxford University Press, 2009).

18. www.wedmagazine.co.uk/vintage-styling-a-regency-romance.html

19. Another reason why many people who call themselves fans of Jane Austen focus more on watching the films and

television dramatizations, rather than on reading the books themselves, is that our society is to some extent losing the ability to read – certainly the ability to read literary novels. I was invited recently to attend a U3A (University of the Third Age) reading group, to talk about Jane Austen. As the group identified themselves as a reading group made up of retired women, I suggested that they read a Jane Austen novel in advance of my visit – and I chose *Persuasion* as it is one of her shorter and more accessible books, and one that often speaks particularly to older women. As I talked with this group, I was astounded to hear how hard they had found the book to read, and how much most of them professed to dislike it. Almost all of them claimed to be Jane Austen fans, but this interest was formed, it transpired, only from the films and TV serializations. A very helpful conversation developed in which we all came to realize that the majority of the books that are particularly promoted to reading groups are very plot-driven and easy to read, and that many of us have lost the habit of reading more classical or literary books. Such books often demand more work from a reader, as he or she needs to absorb more detail about background, take in more reflection on a character's inner journey, and engage with rich, but often long and complex, sentences – work that in a film the director will do for us with very little effort required on the part of the viewer. This concern has been recognized more widely, and the concept of Slow Reading is being advocated by many to reduce stress in our fast-moving, ever-busy world and to restore the pleasure of reading for itself, not just to discover what happens at the end of the story.

Appendix

1.   R. W. Chapman (ed.), *Minor Works*, pp. 453–57.

Select Bibliography

Writings of Jane Austen:

Novels:
Sense and Sensibility, first published 1811
Pride and Prejudice, first published 1813
Mansfield Park, first published 1814
Emma, first published 1816
Northanger Abbey, first published 1818
Persuasion, first published 1818
Other writings:
Minor Works [MW], collected and edited by R. W. Chapman (Oxford: Oxford University Press, first published 1954; revised edition 1989)

Letters:
Jane Austen's Letters, Brabourne Edition, first published 1884
www.pemberley.com/janeinfo/brablt15.html
Jane Austen's Letters, collected and edited by Deirdre Le Faye, (Oxford: Oxford University Press, 2011 [Fourth Edition])

Select list of books relating to Jane Austen, her times, and her world:

Adkins, Roy and Lesley, *Eavesdropping on Jane Austen's England* (London: Abacus, 2014)

Austen, Caroline, *My Aunt Jane Austen: A Memoir* (Winchester: Jane Austen Society, 1991)

Austen-Leigh, J. E., *A Memoir of Jane Austen and Other Family Recollections* (Oxford: Oxford University Press, 2002)

Byrne, Paula, *The Real Jane Austen* (London: William Collins, 2013)

Cecil, David, *A Portrait of Jane Austen* (Harmondsworth: Penguin, 1978)

Collingwood, Jeremy and Margaret, *Hannah More* (Oxford: Lion, 1990)

Collins, Irene, *Jane Austen and the Clergy* (London: The Hambledon Press, 2002)

Collins, Irene, *Jane Austen: The Parson's Daughter* (London: The Hambledon Press, 1998)

Cowper, William, *Selected Poems*, Everyman's Poetry Edition, edited by Michael Bruce (London: J. M. Dent, 1999)

Emsley, Sarah, *Jane Austen's Philosophy of the Virtues* (Palgrave Macmillan, 2005)

Fordyce, James, *Sermons to Young Women* (1766)

Harman, Claire, *Jane's Fame: How Jane Austen Conquered the World* (Edinburgh: Canongate, 2009)

Hill, Constance, *Jane Austen: Her Homes and Her Friends* (London and New York: John Lane, 1923)

Hubback, J. H. and E. C., *Jane Austen's Sailor Brothers* (London and New York: John Lane, 1906)

Jarvis, William, *Jane Austen and Religion* (Oxford: The Stonesfield Press, 1996)

Lane, Maggie, *A Charming Place: Bath in the Life and Novels of Jane Austen* (Bath: Millstream Books, 1988)

Lane, Maggie, *Jane Austen's World: The Life and Times of England's Most Popular Author* (London: Carlton Books, 1996)

Le Faye, Deirdre (ed.), *Jane Austen: A Family Record* (London: The British Library, 1989)

Nokes, David, *Jane Austen: A Life* (New York: Farrar, Straus, and Giroux, 1997)

Russell, Anthony, *The Clerical Profession* (London: SPCK, 1980)

Russell, Anthony, *The Country Parish* (London: SPCK, 1986)

Todd, Janet (ed.), *Jane Austen in Context* (Cambridge: Cambridge University Press, 2005)

Tomalin, Claire, *Jane Austen: A Life* (London: Viking, 1997)

Tucker, George Holbert, *A Goodly Heritage: A History of Jane Austen's Family* (Stroud: Sutton Publishing Ltd, 1998)

Uglow, Jenny, *In These Times: Living in Britain through Napoleon's Wars 1793 – 1815* (London: Faber and Faber, 2015)

Wheeler, Michael, *Jane Austen and Winchester Cathedral* (Winchester: Friends of Winchester Cathedral, 2003)

Select list of books relating to literary and academic criticism of Jane Austen:

Butler, Marilyn, *Jane Austen and the War of Ideas* (Oxford: Clarendon Press, 1987)

Drabble, Margaret (ed.), "Introduction", in *Lady Susan, The Watsons, Sanditon* (London: Penguin, 1974)

Lascelles, Mary, *Jane Austen and Her Art* (Oxford: Oxford University Press, 1939)

Southam, Brian (ed.), *Jane Austen: The Critical Heritage* (London: Routledge & Kegan Paul, 1968)

Tanner, Tony, "Introduction", in *Mansfield Park* (London: Penguin English Library, 1966)

Tanner, Tony, *Jane Austen* (Basingstoke: Macmillan, 1986)

Todd, Janet, *The Cambridge Introduction to Jane Austen* (Cambridge: Cambridge University Press, 2006)

Select list of other useful books relating to themes in this book:

Bebbington, D. W., *Evangelicalism in Modern Britain* (London: Unwin Hyman, 1989)

Foster, Richard, *Streams of Living Water: Essential Practices from the Six Great Traditions of Christian Faith* (New York: HarperSan Francisco, 1998)

Fowler, Karen Joy, *The Jane Austen Book Club* (London: Viking, 2004)

Gant, Andrew, *O Sing unto the Lord: A History of English Church Music* (London: Profile Books, 2015)

Gaskell, Elizabeth, *The Life of Charlotte Brontë* (Oxford: Oxford University Press, 2009)

Gordon, James M., *Evangelical Spirituality* (London: SPCK, 1991)

Grahame-Smith, Seth, *Pride and Prejudice and Zombies* (Philadelphia, PA: Quirk Books, 2009)

Jenkyns, Richard, *Westminster Abbey* (London: Profile Books Ltd, 2011)

Kipling, Rudyard, *Rudyard Kipling's Verse: The Definitive Edition* (London: Hodder and Stoughton, 1940)

Mursell, Gordon, *English Spirituality from 1700 to the Present Day* (London: SPCK, 2008)

MacIntyre, Alasdair, *After Virtue: A Study in Moral Theology* (London: Bloomsbury, 2007 [Third Edition])

Moritz, Karl, *Travels in England in 1782*, Chapter Four (Full transcript at www.visionofbritain.org.uk/travellers/Moritz)

Neill, Stephen, *Anglicanism* (London: Mowbray, 1977 [Fourth Edition])

Plumb, J. H., *England in the Eighteenth Century (1714 – 1815)* (London: Penguin, 1961)

Said, Edward, *Culture and Imperialism* (London: Vintage, 1993)

Vidler, Alec R., *The Church in an Age of Revolution* (London: Penguin, 1990)

Watt, Ian, *The Rise of the Novel: Studies in Defoe, Richardson and Fielding* (London: Chatto and Windus, 1957)

Wright, Tom, *Virtue Reborn* (London: SPCK, 2010)

The Austen Project:

McDermid, Val, *Northanger Abbey* (London: HarperCollins, 2014)

McCall Smith, Alexander, *Emma* (London: HarperCollins, 2014)

Sittenfeld, Curtis, *Eligible* (London: HarperCollins, 2016)

Trollope, Joanna, *Sense and Sensibility* (London: HarperCollins, 2013)

Film and TV:

Pride and Prejudice (1940) Directed by Robert Z. Leonard [Film]. United States: MGM

Pride and Prejudice (1980) BBC, 13 January

Mansfield Park (1983) BBC, 6 November

Persuasion (1995) BBC, 16 April

Pride and Prejudice (1995) BBC, 24 September

Mansfield Park (2000) Directed by Patricia Rozema [Film]. London: Miramax

Pride and Prejudice (2005) Directed by Joe Wright [Film]. London: Working Title Films

Mansfield Park (2007) ITV, 18 March

The Jane Austen Book Club (2007). Directed by Robin Swicord [Film]. United States: Sony

Pride and Prejudice and Zombies (2016). Directed by Burr Steers [Film]. London: Lionsgate

INDEX

Other titles from

LION BOOKS

THE FAITH OF
WILLIAM SHAKESPEARE

Graham Holderness

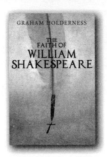

"A very powerful case."
Dr Rowan Williams

William Shakespeare stills stands head and shoulders above any other author in the English language, a position that is unlikely ever to change. Yet it is often said that we know very little about him – and that applies as much to what he believed as it does to the rest of his biography. Or does it?

In this authoritative new study, Graham Holderness takes us through the context of Shakespeare's life, the times of religious and political turmoil, and looks at what we do know of Shakespeare the Anglican. But then he goes beyond that, and mines the plays themselves, not just for the words of the characters, but for the concepts, themes and language which Shakespeare was himself steeped in – the language of the Bible and *The Book of Common Prayer*.

Considering particularly such plays as *Richard II*, *Henry V*, *The Merchant of Venice*, *Measure for Measure*, *Hamlet*, *Othello*, *The Tempest* and *The Winter's Tale*, Holderness shows how the ideas of Catholicism come up against those of Luther and Calvin; how Christianity was woven deep into Shakespeare's psyche, and how he brought it again and again to his art.

ISBN: 978-0-7459-6891-9 | e-ISBN: 978-0-7459-6892-6

CHARLES DICKENS
FAITH, ANGELS AND THE POOR

Keith Hooper

PUBLISHING MAY 2017

Charles Dickens was a great storyteller whose influence and reach extended beyond that normally associated with a novelist. A journalist, commentator, historian, and the social conscience of a nation, Dickens possessed the rare ability of documenting the realities of life, and his novels have both challenged and entertained his contemporaries and posterity.

But what of Dickens' beliefs? And what did Dickens hope to communicate through his writings to an audience that would continue beyond his lifetime?

Keith Hooper explores how Charles Dickens tried through his work to change the hearts of his readers. By exploring the nature and development of Dickens's faith, and the means by which it was expressed, we gain new and valuable insight into his literary work.

There are many books out there on Charles Dickens, but none that seek to understand what his faith meant to him, how it was reflected in his writings, or how he struggled with the church of his time.

ISBN: 978-0-7459-6851-3 | e-ISBN: 978-0-7459-6852-0

THE THOMAS
THE TANK ENGINE MAN

Brian Sibley

"With this book, you are definitely on
the right track. So, climb aboard.
And – 'Tickets please!'"
Gyles Brandreth

The stories of Thomas the Tank Engine and his friends have
delighted generations of children and adults. First published
as wonderfully illustrated books they spawned a host of games,
television series, DVDs and a range of other merchandise.

But what do we know of the Reverend W. Awdry who started
telling the stories to amuse his own children, with no idea that
the characters would lead to a global phenomenon?

In this fascinating and warm biography, Brian Sibley brings
to life one of the most eminent children's writers of the twentieth
century. From his Edwardian childhood to World War II and
beyond, Sibley reveals Awdry as a man of courage and shows
why – with Thomas and his friends – he continues to charm
both adults and children alike throughout the world.

Hardback ISBN: 978-0-7459-7027-1
Paperback ISBN: 978-0-7459-7029-5
e-ISBN: 978-0-7459-7028-8

THE
OXFORD INKLINGS

Colin Duriez

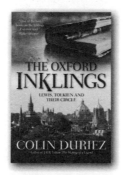

"One of the best books on the Inklings I've ever read."
Walter Hooper

The Oxford Inklings tells the story of the friendships, mutual influence, and common purpose of the Inklings – the literary circle which congregated around C.S. Lewis and J.R.R. Tolkien.

Meeting in pubs or Lewis's college rooms, they included an influential array of literary figures. They were, claimed poet and novelist John Wain, bent on "the task of redirecting the whole current of contemporary art and life".

Tolkien and Lewis expert Colin Duriez unpacks the Inklings' origins, relationships, and the nature of their collaboration. He shows how they influenced, encouraged, and moulded each other. Duriez also covers the less celebrated Inklings, neglected, he claims, for too long. What did they owe – and offer – to the more acknowledged names? What brought them together? And what, eventually, drove them apart from their initial focus upon each other's writings?

ISBN: 978-0-7459-5631-3 | e-ISBN: 978-0-7459-5792-0

C.S. LEWIS
A BIOGRAPHY OF FRIENDSHIP

Colin Duriez

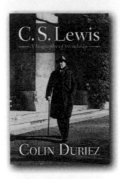

"A fine contribution to our understanding of a great man."
Dr Rowan Williams

You can learn a great deal about people by their friends, never more so than in the case of C.S. Lewis: the remarkable academic, populariser of faith, and creator of Narnia.

Key relationships mattered deeply to him, and profoundly influenced his beliefs and writings – a life-long childhood friend, his gifted but alcoholic brother, J.R.R. Tolkien and the other Inklings, a single mother twice his age, and his beloved Joy, whom he married late in life. In this sparkling new biography, which draws on material not previously published, Colin Duriez brings C.S. Lewis and these friendships to life.

ISBN: 978-0-7459-5587-2 | e-ISBN: 978-0-7459-5725-8

THE A–Z OF
C.S. LEWIS

Colin Duriez

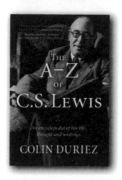

"This is one of the most useful books I know.
I look for excuses to read it."
Walter Hooper

The A–Z of C.S. Lewis is a comprehensive introduction to C.S. Lewis's life, family, friends, career, marriage, and writings, and also to the worlds he created, the creatures he imagined, and the studies he delighted in. Whether you are a devotee of all things Lewis, or just beginning to explore him and his world, this guide is for you.

ISBN: 978-0-7459-5586-5 | e-ISBN: 978-0-7459-5789-0

J.R.R. TOLKIEN
THE MAKING OF A LEGEND

Colin Duriez

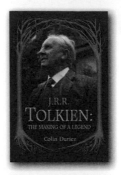

"[A] well-researched and highly readable biography."
Brian Sibley

Long before the successful *The Lord of the Rings* films, J.R.R. Tolkien's creations, imagination, and characters had captured the attention of millions of readers. But who was the man who dreamt up the intricate languages and perfectly crafted world of Middle-earth?

Tolkien had a difficult life for many years: orphaned and poor, his guardian forbad him to communicate with the woman he had fallen in love with, and he went through the horrors of the First World War. An intensely private and brilliant scholar, he spent over fifty years working on the languages, history, peoples, and geography of Middle-earth, with a consistent mythology inspired by a formidable knowledge of early northern European history and culture. J.R.R. Tolkien became a legend by creating an imaginary world that has enthralled and delighted generations. This engaging and accessible biography brings him to life.

ISBN: 978-0-7459-5514-8 | e-ISBN: 978-0-7459-5709-8

JOHN MUIR

Mary Colwell

"Read this and meet the man whose writing, commitment, and integrity persuaded a president that nature matters."
Professor Tim Birkhead FRS

Throughout his life, John Muir was a passionate believer that everyone needs a place to play, and some places were just too special to be destroyed for money.

Born in Scotland in 1838, the celebrated naturalist had a harsh childhood, yet he fell irrevocably in love with the world around him. After emigrating to America, he grew up with a passion for nature and its Maker, becoming a founding father of the National Parks of America. A skilled and ingenious inventor, a superb writer and a fearless explorer, he found his heaven on earth in the Sierra Nevada mountains. He was the founder and first President of the Sierra Club.

ISBN: 978-0-7459-5666-4 | e-ISBN: 978-0-7459-5667-1

STARGAZERS

Allan Chapman

"A much needed radical addition to the
prevailing notions of the Enlightenment."
Melvyn Bragg

The period from 1500–1700 saw an unprecendented renaissance
in astronomy and the understanding of the heavens.

In this magnificent tour de force, scientific historian Dr Allan
Chapman guides us through two hundred years of mapping the
stars. He shows how Copernicus, Galileo, Tycho Brahe, and
Kepler were all part of a huge movement, which included many
churchmen, questing for knowledge of the skies.

Chapman explores whether Galileo and his ilk were so
unusual for their time, bright sparks of knowledge in a sea of
ignorance. Or were contemporary Popes, churchmen, and
rulers actually fascinated by astronomy, and open to new ideas?

Within these pages Copernicus and Galileo find company
with Jesuit missionary astronomers in China, Calvinist
physicists in Leiden, Bishop John Wilkins's "Flying Chariot"
destined for the moon, Johannes Hevelius, Jeremiah Horrocks,
Robert Hooke, Sir Isaac Newton, the early Royal Society,
and the Revd James Bradley, who finally detected the earth's
motion in space in 1728.

ISBN: 978-0-7459-5627-5 | e-ISBN: 978-0-7459-5787-6

PHYSICIANS, PLAGUES AND PROGRESS

Allan Chapman

Since the dawn of time, man has sought to improve his health and that of his neighbour. The human race, around the world, has been on a long and complex journey, seeking to find out how our bodies work, and what heals them.

Embarking on a four-thousand-year odyssey, science historian Allan Chapman brings to life the origin and development of medicine and surgery. Writing with pace and rigorous accuracy, he investigates how we have battled against injury and disease, and provides a gripping and highly readable account of the various victories and discoveries along the way.

Drawing on sources from across Europe and beyond, Chapman discusses the huge contributions to medicine made by the Greeks, the Romans, the early medieval Arabs, and above all by Western Christendom, looking at how experiment, discovery, and improving technology impact upon one another to produce progress.

This is a fascinating, insightful read, enlivened with many colourful characters and memorable stories of inspired experimenters, theatrical surgeons, student pranks, body-snatchers, "mad-doctors", quacks, and charitable benefactors.

ISBN: 978-0-7459-6895-7 | e-ISBN: 978-0-7459-7040-0

DAVID LIVINGSTONE

Stephen Tomkins

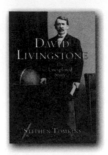

David Livingstone has gone down in history as a fearless explorer and missionary, hacking his way through the forests of Africa to bring light to the people – and also to free them from slavery. But who was he, and what was he actually like?

"He was an extraordinary character" according to biographer Stephen Tomkins "spectacularly bad at personal relationships, at least with white people, possessed of infinite self-belief, courage, and restlessness. He was an almost total failure as a missionary, and so became an explorer and campaigner against the slave trade, hoping to save African lives and souls that way instead. He helped, however unwittingly, to set the tone and the extent of British involvement in Africa. He was a flawed but indomitable idealist."

Fascinating new evidence about Livingstone's life and his struggles have come to light in the letters and journals he left behind, now accessible to us for the first time through spectral imaging. These form a significant addition to the source material for this excellent biography, which provides an honest and balanced account of the real man behind the Victorian icon.

ISBN: 978-0-7459-5568-1 | e-ISBN: 978-0-7459-5719-7